T1-BKG-501

SIMPLE COLONIAL FURNITURE

Colonial Mantel Clock (See page 106)

Simple
Colonial Furniture

By FRANKLIN H. GOTTSHALL

BONANZA BOOKS · NEW YORK

COPYRIGHT, © MCMXXXI-MCMXXXV

THE BRUCE PUBLISHING COMPANY

PRINTED IN THE UNITED STATES OF AMERICA

(Revised Edition)

This edition published by Bonanza Books,
a division of Crown Publishers, Inc.,
by arrangement with the author
F G H

FOREWORD

AT THE present time there is a great interest in colonial furniture. This interest shows itself not only in our homes but also in our schools and is as it should be, for what is more fitting than that American homes should be fitted with distinctly American furniture? The American youth should study American traditions in furniture making as well as in history. One of the greatest factors in raising American antiques to their present high value is the association of them with the daily life of people and events that are now history.

This book is presented as a reference and textbook on early American furniture design and construction. There seems to be very little available material dealing with early American design that is practical for use by craftsmen and students in high schools, normal schools, and vocational schools. This is so because the subject has been presented from the standpoint of reproducing, of copying instead of creating.

The material as developed in these pages is practical for the beginner as well as the experienced craftsman. This is possible only when the designs are created instead of copied.

All the designs suggested are new, but hold very closely to the principles of early American design and construction. All the problems are practical as well as attractive—two factors necessary in the home and school shops to create and hold interest.

Every piece has a bill of material following the description and directions for making. The sizes given are finished sizes, and enough must be added to the length, width, and thickness of the stock to allow for the dressing to size and squaring. In each of these bills of material the thickness is given first, then the width, and lastly the length.

The author wishes to express his thanks and appreciation to the following men who have, by their kindness, helped to make this book possible; to Mr. Guy Reinert of Boyertown, Pa., for offering suggestions and assisting in checking the drawings; to Mr. Frank Spindler of Mt. Berry, Ga., for reading and correcting the text; and to Mr. O. Eugene Wheeler of Atlanta, Ga., for the pen-and-ink sketches which have helped to make the book more attractive and helpful.

To

WALLACE NUTTING

*Whose kindly teaching and early guidance
inspired this book*

CONTENTS

PART I
FURNITURE DESIGN

SIMPLE COLONIAL FURNITURE

ESSENTIALS OF COLONIAL FURNITURE

Life in the early colonies was simple. The character developed in the colonists by continual strife and close contact with a soil that grudgingly yielded them a livelihood, was straightforward and genuine. The hardships and continual struggles necessary to sustain them in a new country, bred in them qualities of simplicity and resourcefulness. These qualities found expression in their institutions, their architecture, and what concerns us more in this book, in their furniture and household furnishings. So well did they plan and build their furniture that today it is more highly esteemed than anything that has been developed to succeed it. Examples of colonial furniture serve us as excellent models that will in all probability be difficult to improve upon for some time to come.

Most colonial furniture, made prior to 1725, was adapted from the Jacobean and even earlier European forms. After that it was influenced by the work of all the great Georgian designers and cabinetmakers. In this connection two things should be noted by the designer: The first and most important is that the designs were usually simplified by the colonists. Thus, for example, the cumbersome, ornate, and exceedingly high bedsteads commonly used in England were simplified and were made in forms similar to the ones shown in this book. Second, the changes in furniture styles were usually several years late in reaching the colonies. This was especially true before the beginning of the eighteenth century. Thus the Georgian styles were already well established in England when Queen Anne designs were just beginning to be adopted by colonial cabinetmakers.

The changes which the colonists made in adapting the European models to their own needs were sometimes nothing more than a change in the wood used, but often they were changes that made the furniture more practical and, therefore, better. Due to the fact that in New England and Pennsylvania most of the early furniture was made by home craftsmen, it was only natural that, although it closely followed European prototypes, a distinct and practical style soon developed, which for want of a better name has been called "colonial." It should be added that the colonial period includes any furniture made in the colonies between the time of the landing of the Mayflower and the close of the eighteenth century.

THREE ESSENTIALS OF DESIGN

Design plays such an important part in the practicability and beauty of a piece of furniture that it will be well, for the beginner especially, to gain a clear idea of what constitutes good design and good construction.

Three things of primary importance must be considered in designing any piece of furniture. They are *utility*, *strength*, and *beauty*. When a piece of furniture has these three qualities, it may truly be said to be well designed. For a clear understanding of how these qualities may be achieved it will be necessary to consider each in turn.

UTILITY IN FURNITURE

One of the things to be considered then, in designing furniture, is utility. How may we gain it? By observing the following rules:

1. Any furniture that is to be built should fulfill a definite need in the home. All other considerations should be secondary or at least not detrimental to the fulfillment of the end.

2. It should be in perfect harmony in design, material, and color with the other furniture in the room. By this is not meant that it must be of the same style or period necessarily, but a sense of fitness must exist.

3. It should be of a suitable size and style so it will fit into its place in the room in a natural manner, without causing either it or the room to seem out of proportion.

4. It should be conducive to comfort, efficiency, and good living, and the design should sincerely express the purpose for which the piece is intended. Let the reader take any piece in this book as a lesson in point. Before making a piece of furniture it is necessary to ask these questions: Will it fulfill a definite need? Will it be in harmony with the rest of the furniture in the room?

STRENGTH IN DESIGN

Furniture should be strong. It should be planned to last, not only through a lifetime, but for several centuries. It is important, therefore, that a designer be a cabinetmaker as well. He must know all about joints and about methods of bracing and fastening pieces together so as to get the sturdiest possible construction. This would be a comparatively simple matter if the important element of beauty could be ignored. But beauty is the element which gives value to furniture, and therefore, is essential. The fact is that, in most instances, we must hide the construction just as a builder and architect must hide the skeleton construction of a frame house or steel building. That is where the difficulty lies —to hide the elements of construction and at the same time make them sufficiently strong. Because the construction can be hidden, and because beauty enhances value, the former element is sacrificed to the interest of the latter in much manufactured furniture. When a cabinetmaker uses small dowels to join a flat stretcher, or a brace to the legs of a large table, because it is cheaper to do so than to mortise and tenon the parts, he is sacrificing strength. When strength is sacrificed, utility and beauty are endangered. When the table comes apart or breaks, where are utility and beauty?

The pieces shown in this book have several peculiarities of construction not generally found in present-day furniture. The principles of construction insisted upon are sound, and are intended to give the greatest possible amount of strength as well as of beauty.

Joints play such an important part in furniture making that it will be well to study them carefully. The joints most widely used in cabinetmaking may be divided into five general headings. They are: (1) the glue joint; (2) the butt joint, which includes the miter joint; (3) the mortise-and-tenon joint, which includes the tongue-and-groove joint; (4) the dovetail joint; (5) the dowel joint. Each of these types is used in making the furniture shown in this book. The student should thoroughly familiarize himself with joints and their applications from a book on the elements of cabinetmaking.

The dowel joint is often misused. Because it is easy and cheap to make, it is often used as an inferior substitute for the mortise-and-tenon joint, especially in making the cheaper types of upholstered-furniture frames and many other types of cabinet construction. It should never be used to fasten a stretcher or an apron to a leg, because it is not strong enough, and comes apart easily. Dowels are correctly used in fastening finials, turned chair rungs, and such other parts as bear no great stress or load. Where the dowel can be made large enough, as in fastening the foot to the X-Stretcher Lowboy Table, its use is permissible. Most of the strains exerted on this joint should tend to hold it in place. In the case of turned chair rungs, it is the only practical joint, though not the most desirable.

The dovetail joint is the most satisfactory for fastening drawers together, but great skill is required to fit it. In early American work, where all dovetails were made by hand, the angle used to lay out dovetails usually was 11 degrees. Dovetails on early work were made a great deal wider than the space between. In machine-made dovetails, the space is as wide as the dovetail.

The mortise-and-tenon joint is the strongest and best joint yet devised for fastening stretchers and rails to legs or stiles. If it is well fitted, the tenon filling the mortise, well glued, and if possible pinned, the joint will last almost indefinitely. It will withstand great strains in every direction. The mortise-and-tenon joints on the pieces in this book are designed, where possible, in such a way that the joint will be flush on the outside. There are two good reasons for this, which early cabinetmakers recognized.

First, where two stretchers are fastened to a leg at right angles to each other, longer tenons are possible, allowing more glued surface and a bigger and stronger joint; second, a flush joint is easy to clean and smooth after having been assembled. These two considerations, having to do

with strength and beauty, are of vital importance in a joint.

Where an especially strong and durable joint is necessary, the mortise-and-tenon joint should also be pinned. To do this, proceed as follows: Glue and clamp the joint. While the clamps are still in place, bore ¼-inch round holes about ⅜ inch from the shoulder into the mortised piece. Into this, drive square or roughly octagoned pegs which are as wide across the flat sides as the diameter of the hole. Before driving the peg, sharpen it at one end and apply glue. Drive the peg deep enough so it will pass through the tenon and into the opposite wall of the mortise. Make the peg or pin long enough so that its head may be trimmed even with the face of the piece into which it has been driven. Use only straight-grained hard wood to make pegs.

Many cabinetmakers claim that a glued mortise-and-tenon joint is strong enough without the peg, and that the ends of the pegs spoil the appearance of the furniture. It is but necessary to look about in practically any home to see that glued mortise-and-tenon joints do not always hold. A sudden and severe shock will often jar a mortise-and-tenon joint loose. The peg prevents this. An examination of some of the finest pieces in museums, pieces of recognized excellence, will prove that pins were used and do not mar their beauty.

The butt joint and glue joint need very little, if any, discussion here. Every novice in cabinetmaking is familiar with them.

BEAUTY IN FURNITURE

Beauty is of paramount importance in furniture. Almost anyone who is handy with tools may build a table or chair which has a maximum of utility and strength. But strength is not all that is desired in a table or chair. An oak library table of the kind commonly found in mail-order catalogs, well made and nicely finished, may be bought for $20 or $25. It will have square legs, straight stretchers, and may even be stronger than the library table shown in this book, which, however, is worth two or three times that price. Which is the more desirable, and what makes it more desirable? Beauty of course; not strength or utility. People seek beauty in their architecture, in their automobile, in their furniture, and pay higher prices to get it. Beauty is the greatest factor in determining the value of furniture as well as of many other things.

It is difficult to analyze beauty. In viewing a piece of furniture most people cannot pick out the distinct qualities or combination of qualities which please the eye and delight the mind. Generally speaking, the most important elements of beauty in a piece of furniture are (*a*) pleasing form, (*b*) correct proportion, (*c*) balance. Excellent materials, good color, brilliance of finish and fitness in surrounding also are elements of beauty. Some of these are

more or less included in the three elements first enumerated.

PLEASING FORM

We may take it for granted that pleasing form in a piece of furniture will cause it to attract favorable attention, and is, therefore, one of the ends to be sought.

1. In developing the form of a piece of furniture, the first essential is the division of the entire unit into a dominant or primary mass and minor masses which are overshadowed in size and interest by the former. Both major and minor masses may be divided again into parts or units according to need, but again these subdivisions will of necessity be unequal and will repeat the principle of dominant and minor division. The desk on page 96 illustrates the principle just stated. The base as a whole is the dominant mass and the top is the minor mass. The base again is divided into a dominant middle section (a void, it is true) and minor side sections. When the top is opened, the arrangement of pigeon holes

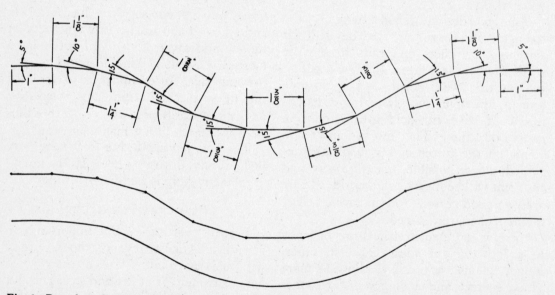

Fig. 1. Procedure that may be followed in plotting a beautiful curve of the type found in the curved apron of the Slant-Top Secretary. The angles may be varied or they may remain the same, as the case may require. The same holds true of the length of the lines. Thus it may be seen that the possibilities of variety are endless.

and drawers, it will be noted, repeats the underlying dominant arrangement.

2. Pleasing form may be attained by careful combinations of straight lines and curves. This is well illustrated in the hood of the Colonial Mantel Clock. The curved lines seem to give the design a freedom from restraint that would hardly be possible with straight lines alone.

3. Logical construction is an important factor in securing pleasing form. The beauty of a design, as well as its fitness, depends largely on this vital factor. If the structural lines of a piece of furniture are weak, no amount of surface enrichment is likely to hide it. Thus in the colonial-clock design the lower section rests upon a base wider than itself, while it, in turn, is wider than the section above it which holds the mechanism. Moreover, capping the upper section is a hood which seems to shelter the rest of the piece. It is logical that a piece such as this should have a cover for the same reason that a house has a roof; for is not this piece a diminutive architectural structure? The quarter columns impart a feeling of strength and stability to the lower section.

4. To have pleasing form a piece of furniture should have rhythm, especially in its curved lines. And this leads us to say a word about the circle which cannot be considered a beautiful curve. The circle is mechanical, and like all mechanical curves lacks interest. It returns to its starting point and, therefore, has not enough variety to hold interest. A curve to have interest must never come back to its starting point but must unfold itself with certain rhythmic measures. For instance, a curve may be plotted by connecting a series of straight lines placed end to end, each line forming an angle with the next one, varying the same number of degrees each time. Each line may be varied in length by cutting off or adding to it the same amount each time.

A curve drawn through the points of intersection will be beautiful. A curve to be beautiful must never seem to hesitate in unfolding itself. A good curve sense must be developed by the designer if he would succeed in his work. He must train himself to draw beautiful curves without the aid of mechanical devices.

5. Pleasing form may be secured or enhanced by surface enrichment. The structure of the object, its shape or position, often suggests the type of enrichment. Thus the pierced and scrolled pieces used to decorate the hood of the Colonial Mantel Clock were suggested partly by the shape of the hood, partly by the need for a type of ornament that would not appear heavy. The designer must be careful lest enrichment makes a piece of furniture seem top-heavy. The scrolled pieces on top of the clock do not do this and are admirable in this respect. Also, he must beware of superfluous ornament, for it tires the eye and destroys that sense of repose so much valued in good furniture design. Enrichment and ornament in order to be successful must not be just added, but must appear to be a part of the piece of the furniture itself.

6. Last of all, simplicity must not be forgotten. It is one of the greatest factors, if not the greatest, whereby pleasing form and true beauty are secured. The Ladder-Back Side Chair, for example, owes most of its charm to its simplicity. Simplicity should be the keynote of colonial furniture design.

CORRECT PROPORTION

Good proportion is secured by a proper relation of mass and space, of lines and surfaces. So important is proportion that a design will be a complete failure without it, though it has all the other elements of beauty. Nor is it possible to lay down a hard-and-fast rule whereby it may be attained. Even the ancient Greeks, who are at once the glory and despair of modern designers, did not succeed in finding a satisfactory rule that could be applied even to buildings. No designer can say: "Here is a table of such and such a size; put on it legs of this diameter and they will be in proportion to the rest of the design." In most pieces of furniture, the basic dimensions cannot be varied very much. The height of the seat of a chair, for instance, does not go far above or much below 18 inches. Such fixed dimensions have an important influence on all proportions of furniture pieces. Since essentially proportion is nothing more than the relation of one dimension to another, it follows that correct proportions can be secured only by the best possible relation of one or several

more or less fixed elements to the variable elements in the piece. Usually this sense of proper relation may be cultivated only by conscientious effort.

Pleasing proportions result when there is a seeming unity brought about by this proper relationship of elements. The proportion of a square, however, while it may seem that it should be harmonious because each of its elements are the same, is not so good as that of most rectangles. Satisfying proportion is not brought about by the relation of identical elements so often as it is by a pleasing arrangement of several elements of unequal value. It may be well to point out, however, that the contrast must not be too great.

In designing a chair, then, the limit of height of the seat must be taken into con-

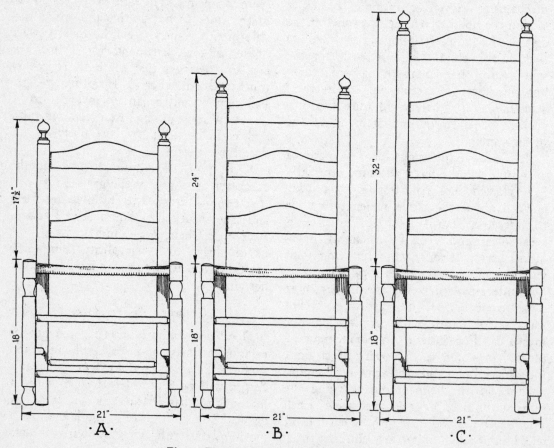

Fig. 2. Designing a Ladder-Back Side Chair

sideration. Suppose that a rectangle is placed vertically on a sheet of paper and in it a distance of 18 inches is measured off in a convenient scale for the height of the seat. Next is chosen a width that will be comfortable in a seat. This will serve for the width of the rectangle. In a side chair, this width may be from 14 to 18 inches at the back of the seat. In armchairs it may be as much as 25 inches. Now the top of the rectangle may be divided experimentally into several divisions until one is found that seems to be more pleasing than the rest. In this way a pleasing height for the back of the chair may be arrived at.

To illustrate these principles definitely, the Ladder-Back Side Chair may be taken as a lesson in point. In Figure 2 are shown three chairs. The lower section of each is alike. In A the chair back is a square. In C the contrast of length to width is too great. In B however, which represents the back of the Ladder-Back Side Chair, the proportion is better. Obviously, it is more pleasing than either A or C.

BALANCE

The quality of balance is secured in a piece of furniture by the proper placing of masses and outlines so that effects of equalization are produced on each side of a given point. This principle is well illustrated in the mantel clock, page 108. For example, the figured veneer on one side of the central mass on the door is balanced by that on the other side. The finial on one side of the hood forms a balanced relation to the one on the opposite side. To place one finial nearer to the center than the other would immediately throw the design out of balance.

Closely related to balance is stability which may be secured by a proper arrangement of masses and supports so that the divisions grow larger or more prominent in a downward direction. The construction and arrangement of the elements in the colonial clock case may again be studied in this respect. A better example might be the chest of drawers, in which the drawer fronts are wider toward the floor. Consider the effect if the arrangement were reversed so that the largest drawer were moved to the top with the smaller ones at the bottom. The piece would at once seem to be upside down.

HARMONY

A last factor toward securing balance is harmony. Harmony is secured by keeping elements properly related to each other, by preventing elements that would clash from being brought too close together. We can think of no better example than that of furnishing a room partly in oak and partly in mahogany furniture or of putting an oak panel into a mahogany door. These are radical examples but they serve to illustrate our point.

THE MECHANICS OF FURNITURE DESIGN

The foregoing paragraphs have outlined the chief characteristics of colonial furniture design. It may be well to add a definite plan for designing a given piece which the home craftsman may want to make.

In designing any piece of furniture a list of requirements and desirable features, like the foregoing, is a distinct help to the novice and occasional designer. It is the best means of preventing the designer from overlooking an essential need.

If, for instance, a table is to be designed, the qualities that are desirable in a table of the type wanted should be listed. A dining table will serve as an example. Some of the qualities of a good dining table are: (1) comfortable height; (2) adequate table surface; (3) harmony of design and material with other furniture in the room; (4) adaptability of size to the family; (5) arrangement of legs and bracing not to interfere with comfort; (6) sincere expression in the design of the purpose for which the table is intended.

The next step is the preparation of preliminary pencil sketches of the proposed piece. These sketches are to be considered as studies which the designer revises and corrects thoughtfully and carefully until he has found the most beautiful and practical expression of his idea.

In developing the sketches for a piece, separate sketches of intricate details, such as aprons, turnings, and difficult joints, are made next. These must be studied quite as carefully as the general sketches to avoid difficulties and failures in construction.

When the rough sketches are completed to include the essential dimensions, a preliminary scale drawing may be made. In this all the curves and shapes and construction details will be accurately shown, and the dimensions will be correctly added. Here again thoughtful attention to both the artistic and practical results, to good methods of construction will contribute to the success of the piece. Since it is not probable that the preliminary scale drawing will be neat or well arranged on the paper, and since there will have been many erasures and changes, it is usually best to make a separate, final scale drawing.

Usually a good scale to use is $3'' = 1'—0''$. Special details may be shown a little larger. A good way to see if all dimensions necessary for making the piece have been included is to make out a bill of material, but without taking off measurements from the drawing with a rule. If any are missing they may be added at this time.

After this has been done, it should be possible to make the piece from the drawing. If the drawing is complete and has been carefully made, all shaped pieces should be shown in such a manner that full-sized patterns can easily be prepared for laying out the design on the wood. (As an example, see the squares drawn to get the pattern of the feet and top on the small mantel clock, page 104.) Some drawings so lack details of joints, or give such inadequate data for performing operations with which the average workman is not familiar, that they are almost useless as guides. A broad knowledge of styles, construction, the use of machinery, familiarity with turning and carving, and above all, a wide and varied experience in the cabinetmaking trade, are valuable assets to the designer.

From a study of the foregoing it is hoped that the home craftsman and student will gain some knowledge that will be of value in an effort to design good furniture. However, it is strongly urged that the worker learn to train himself to look for those things that are desirable and to develop a habit of observation. He should visit museums, historical societies, and other places where good furniture may be studied in collections. In this way he may compare, and to some degree at least, familiarize himself with the good styles and their merits.

PART II

COLONIAL FURNITURE DESIGNS

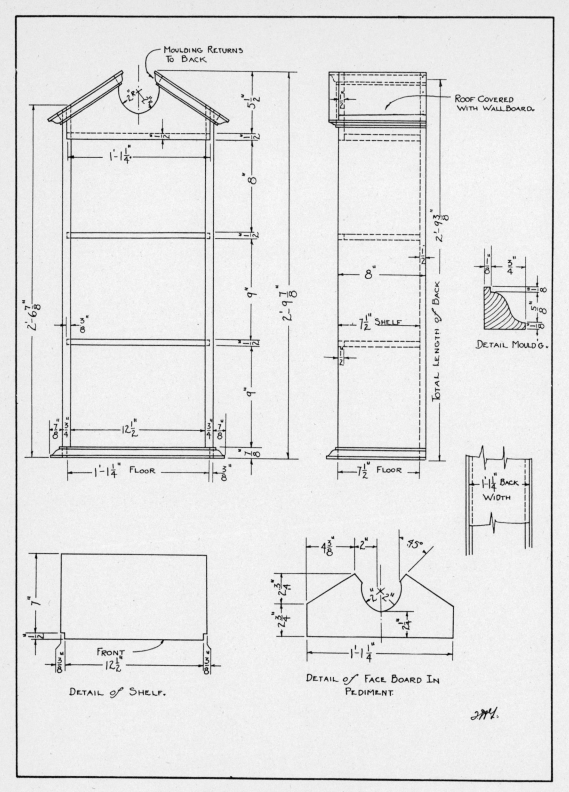

MOULDING RETURNS TO BACK

ROOF COVERED WITH WALLBOARD.

DETAIL MOULD'G.

BACK WIDTH

DETAIL OF SHELF.

FRONT

DETAIL OF FACE BOARD IN PEDIMENT.

Plate 1. Small Wall Bookshelves

SMALL WALL BOOKSHELVES

Small wall bookshelves provide an easy opportunity for the home craftsman and the student of furniture making to begin the successful construction of typical colonial-furniture pieces. The shelves are interesting to make, and at the same time provide the maker with an opportunity to apply his skill in many elementary furniture-making processes. The shelves involve squaring, mitering, the making of a simple pattern (the face board in the pediment), simple mortise-and-tenon cutting and fitting, gluing and assembling, and other basic operations.

BILL OF MATERIAL

Sides	2 pc.	$\frac{3}{4}$ x	8	x 30$\frac{7}{8}$
Shelves	2 pc.	$\frac{1}{2}$ x	7$\frac{1}{2}$	x 13$\frac{1}{4}$
Top	1 pc.	$\frac{1}{2}$ x	7	x 13$\frac{1}{4}$
Face board in pediment	1 pc.	$\frac{1}{2}$ x	5$\frac{1}{2}$	x 13$\frac{1}{4}$
Back		$\frac{1}{2}$ x	13$\frac{1}{4}$	x 33$\frac{3}{8}$
Molding and wall board				
Floor	1 pc.	$\frac{7}{8}$ x	7$\frac{1}{2}$	x 13$\frac{1}{4}$

Fig. 3. Small Wall Bookshelves

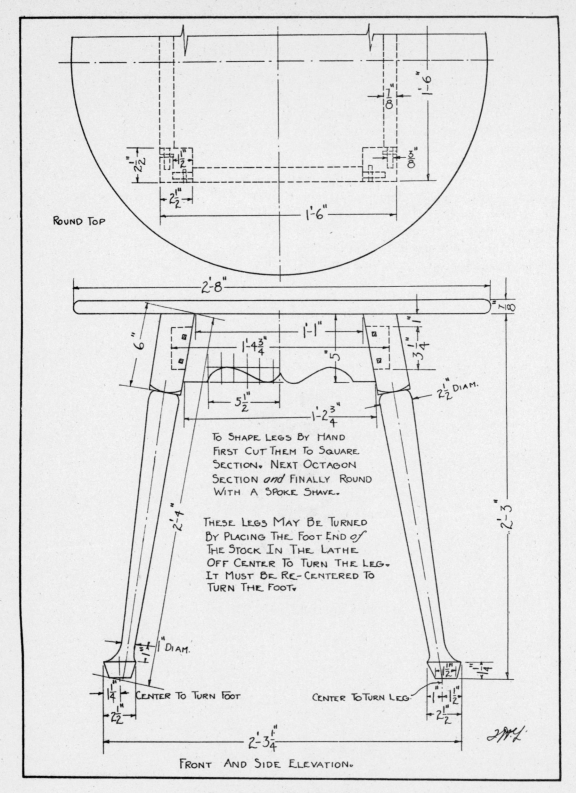

ROUND TOP

TO SHAPE LEGS BY HAND
FIRST CUT THEM TO SQUARE
SECTION. NEXT OCTAGON
SECTION *and* FINALLY ROUND
WITH A SPOKE SHAVE.

THESE LEGS MAY BE TURNED
BY PLACING THE FOOT END *of*
THE STOCK IN THE LATHE
OFF CENTER TO TURN THE LEG.
IT MUST BE RE-CENTERED TO
TURN THE FOOT.

CENTER TO TURN FOOT

CENTER TO TURN LEG

FRONT AND SIDE ELEVATION.

Plate 2. Round-Top Card Table

ROUND-TOP CARD TABLE

The round-top table is a useful piece of furniture and a valuable problem for the beginner in cabinetwork, because it involves several important operations not generally found in ordinary furniture making. One operation is the shaping and forming of splay legs, either by off-center turning in the lathe, or with hand tools. The other is the fitting of this type of legs. The beginner who wishes to have the broadest kind of experience may make the legs for the present table by both the turning and the hand-tool methods.

BILL OF MATERIAL

Legs ------------------4 pc. 2½ x 2½ x 28
Top ------------------1 pc. ⅞ x 32 diam.
Aprons ------------4 pc. ⅞ x 5 x 16¾

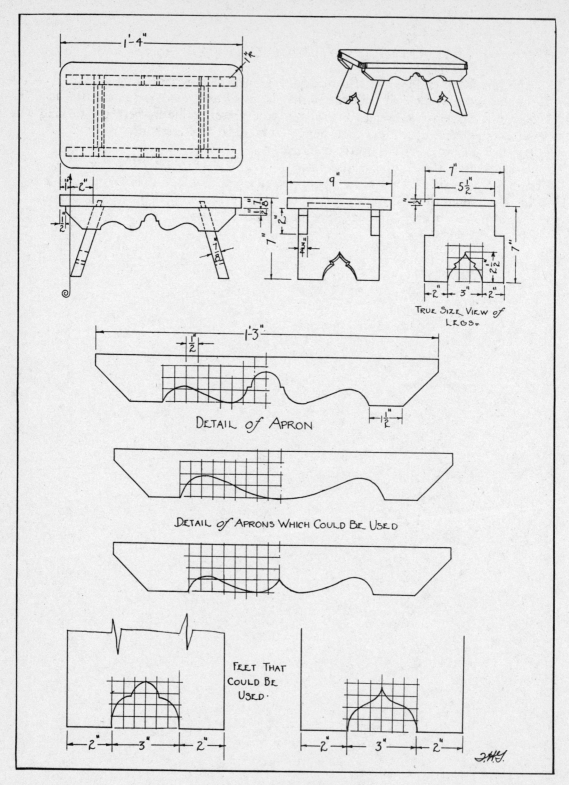

1'-4"

1"R

9"

7"

5½"

7"

2"

½"

2"

7"

2"

2"

TRUE SIZE VIEW OF LEGS.

1'-3"

½"

½"

DETAIL OF APRON

DETAIL OF APRONS WHICH COULD BE USED

FEET THAT COULD BE USED.

2" 3" 2"

2" 3" 2"

Plate 3. Splay-Legged Footstool

SPLAY-LEGGED FOOTSTOOL

The splay-legged footstool is a beginner's problem. It involves such basic processes as coping-saw work, smoothing, squaring, making of patterns, mortising, and tenoning. By taking advantage of different combinations of feet and aprons, as many as eight or nine different variations of the basic design may be made. This variety is attractive to the lover of colonial furniture. The stool has been planned so that the same-sized stock may be used, no matter which patterns are combined.

BILL OF MATERIAL

Top _____1 pc. ⅞ x 9 x 16
Aprons _____2 pc. ¾ x 2 x 15
Legs _____2 pc. ⅞ x 7 x 7½

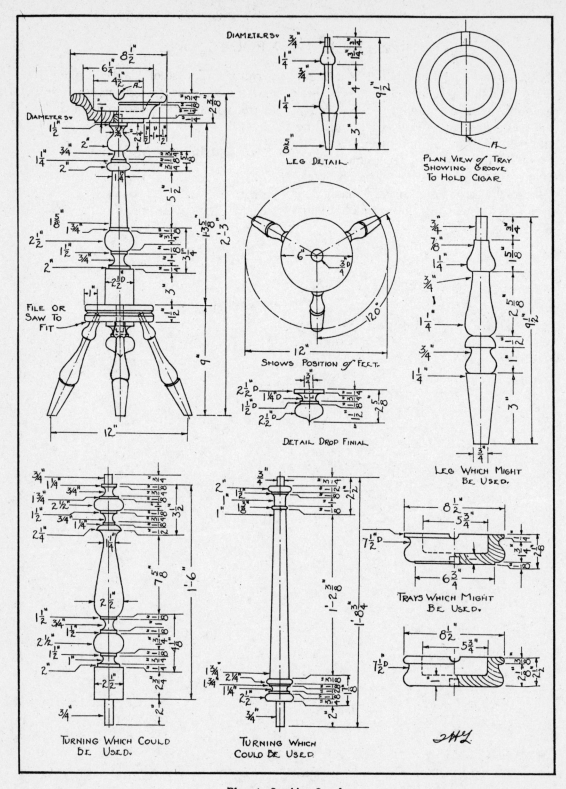

Plate 4. Smoking Stand

SMOKING STAND

Here is a smoking stand that is different. It is a turning problem. By interchanging parts, about twelve different variations of the original design may be made. The size of the stock is the same no matter which style of turning is used. It offers practice in spindle as well as faceplate turning. The dowel on the column is made long enough to pass through the stool seat and hold the drop finial which is glued to it.

BILL OF MATERIAL

Tray	1 pc. 2⅜ x 8½ diam.
Turned column	1 pc. 2½ diam. x 18⅜
Turned legs	3 pc. 1¼ diam. x 9½
Finial	1 pc. 2½ diam. x 2⅝
Round piece to which legs are fastened	1 pc. 1½ x 6 diam.

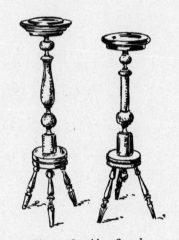

Fig. 4. Smoking Stands

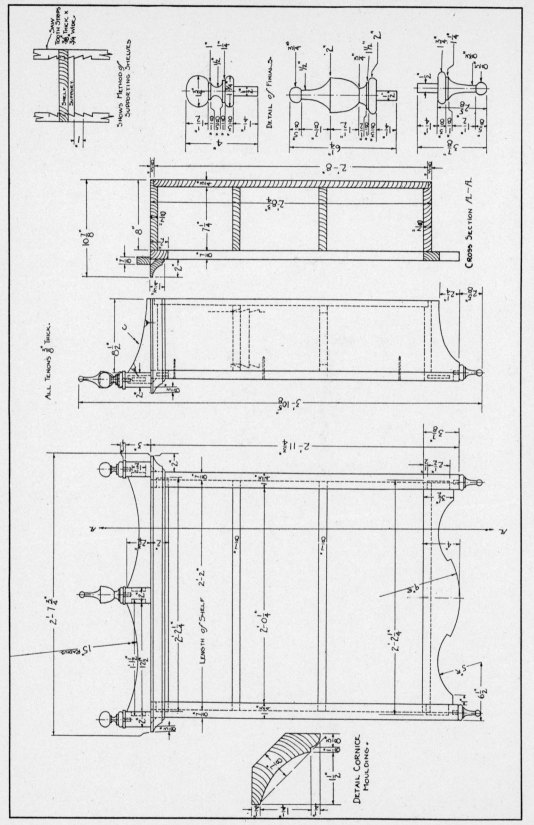

Plate 5. Hanging Wall Bookshelves or Trophy Cabinet

HANGING WALL BOOKSHELVES OR TROPHY CABINET

The cabinet shown in the accompanying drawing may be used as bookshelves or a china cabinet, and will be found excellent for holding trophies in golf tournaments and athletic contests. The cabinet is ideal, not only for home use, but is especially well adapted for schools, colleges, and other public institutions where trophies are preserved.

The cabinet is easy to make; simple, yet elegant. It adapts itself excellently to construction by a group of workers. It is well designed without being "fancy" as are so many wall cabinets.

BILL OF MATERIAL

Top rail of frame __1 pc. $\frac{7}{8}$ x 2 x 26$\frac{1}{4}$
Stiles of frame _____2 pc. $\frac{7}{8}$ x 1$\frac{3}{4}$ x 35$\frac{3}{4}$
Bottom rail of
  frame _____1 pc. $\frac{7}{8}$ x 4 x 26$\frac{1}{4}$
Sides _____2 pc. $\frac{7}{8}$ x 8 x 35$\frac{3}{4}$
Top and bottom____2 pc. $\frac{7}{8}$ x 8 x 26
Shelves _____2 pc. $\frac{7}{8}$ x 7$\frac{1}{4}$ x 26
Pedestals for finials 3 pc. 2 x 2 x 3
Caps for pedestals __3 pc. $\frac{1}{4}$ x 2$\frac{1}{4}$ x 2$\frac{1}{4}$
Boards between
  pedestals (C) _____2 pc. $\frac{7}{8}$ x 2$\frac{3}{4}$ x 8$\frac{1}{2}$
Boards in back of
  pedestals (C) _____2 pc. $\frac{7}{8}$ x 2$\frac{3}{4}$ x 8$\frac{1}{2}$
Finials $\begin{cases} 2 \text{ pc. } 1\frac{3}{4} \text{ diam. x 4} \\ 1 \text{ pc. } 2 \quad \text{diam. x } 6\frac{1}{4} \\ 2 \text{ pc. } 1\frac{3}{4} \text{ diam. x } 3\frac{7}{8} \end{cases}$
Cornice molding about 5 feet
Back _____ $\frac{3}{4}$ x 27 x 32
Saw tooth strips _____4 pc. $\frac{3}{8}$ x $\frac{3}{4}$ x 31
Shelf support strips 4 pc. $\frac{3}{8}$ x $\frac{5}{8}$ x 6$\frac{3}{4}$

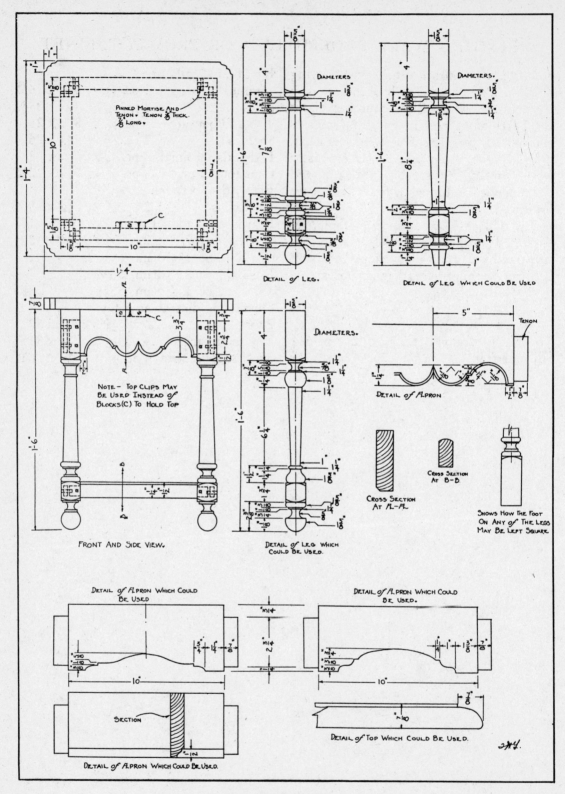

Plate 6. Joint Stool

JOINT STOOL

The joint stool is so called because it is joined together with mortise-and-tenon joints. The colonists, when they first settled in this country, used stools to sit on as much or more than they did chairs, because stools were simpler to make. Very few pieces of furniture are more difficult to make than chairs. Since the early settlers had very little time to make furniture, stools commonly took the place of chairs. Sometimes benches or long forms, as they were called, were used. These were long enough for several persons to sit on side by side. Since nails were difficult to obtain and expensive, the stools always were mortised and tenoned together and pinned.

In order to make them tight, the joints were draw-bored. Clamps probably were scarce in the joiner's shop, and by draw-boring the joints, clamps were not needed.

Fig. 5. Joint Stool

This was done by having the hole through which the peg was to be driven about 1/16 inch closer to the shoulder in the tenon than a corresponding hole bored in the leg. If a peg is driven into such a hole, it will force the shoulder of the horizontal member tightly against the legs.

These pegs were always square or roughly octagoned with a knife. They were never made round for several good reasons. First, the peg was driven into a round hole, the diameter of which was the same as the distance across the flat side of the peg. Thus it fit perfectly tight when driven into the hole. A round peg usually is either too small for the hole, or if it fits tightly, is likely to split the wood. Second the square peg, having corners, makes a path for itself without splitting the wood.

The first operation in making this stool is to turn the legs. The square part on the legs, into which the tenons fasten, should be left sufficiently large so that there will be enough stock to square them up. Great care should also be exercised when turning the feet not to have flat surfaces on them.

Several kinds of legs as well as aprons are shown in the drawing to give variety to the stool. These make it a valuable problem for the home craftsman and for students' first-year work. By using different combinations, as many as twenty different stools can be made from the drawing. The stock sizes are the same, no matter which patterns are used.

BILL OF MATERIAL

Top	1 pc.	7/8 x 16 x 16
Legs	4 pc.	1 5/8 x 1 5/8 x 18
Aprons	4 pc.	7/8 x 3 3/4 x 11 3/4
Crosspieces	4 pc.	7/8 x 1 1/2 x 11 3/4

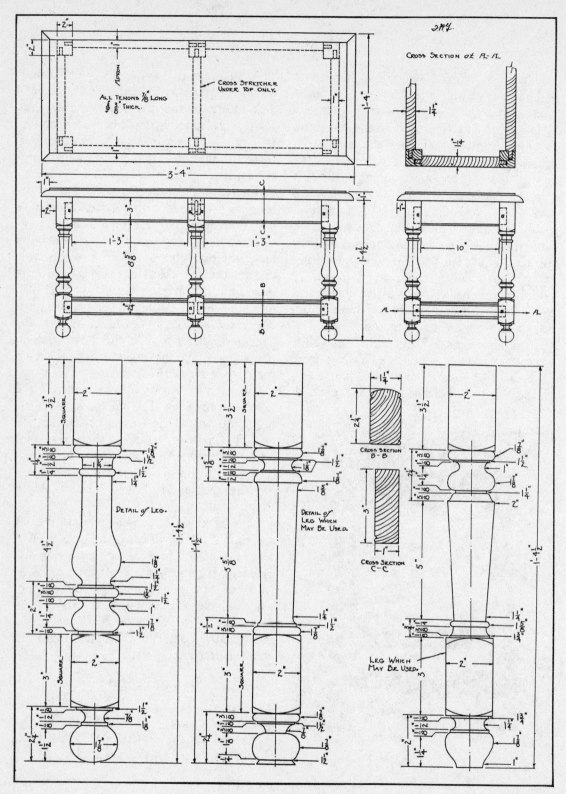

Plate 7. Fireplace Bench

FIREPLACE BENCH

The fireplace bench, as its name implies, is intended to be used in front of the fireplace. It can be used as a piano bench as well, if made about 2 inches higher. If so desired, a cushion seat can be placed upon it and tied to the legs at each corner, to make it more attractive.

Some time ago, benches of this type were made to go with trestle tables or refectory tables. Since these tables usually were quite long, the benches also were made long and were called "long forms." Very often the tops were quite narrow, and the legs were splayed to prevent them from tipping over easily. The long benches almost invariably had stretchers near the floor upon which to rest the feet.

In this bench the legs are not splayed, but the turnings are well shaped and the foot is almost a perfect ball. The bench is sturdily built as well as handsome in appearance.

BILL OF MATERIAL

Top	1 pc. 1	x 16	x 40
Legs	6 pc. 2	x 2	x 16½
End aprons	2 pc. 1	x 3	x 11¾
Side aprons	4 pc. 1	x 3	x 16¾
Cross stretcher under top	1 pc. 1	x 2	x 11¾
Lower end stretchers	2 pc. 1¼	x 2¼	x 11¾
Lower side stretchers	4 pc. 1¼	x 2¼	x 16¾

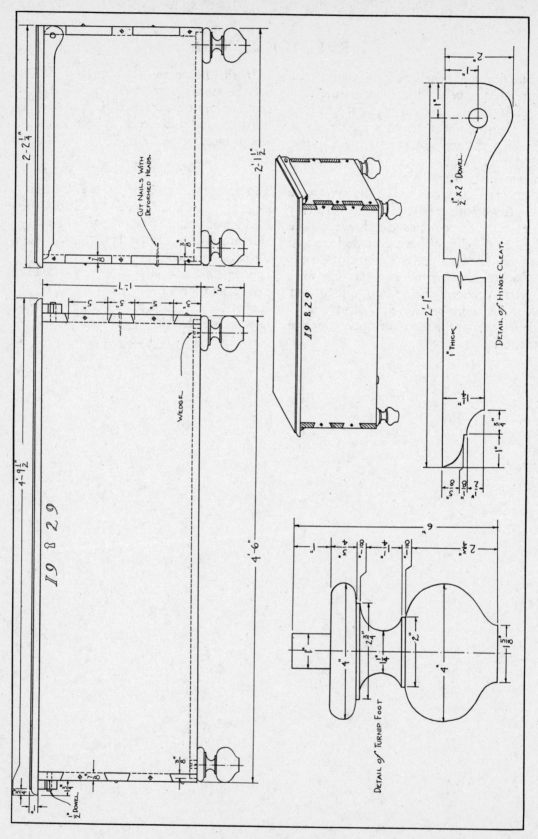

Detail of Hinge Cleat.

Detail of Turnip Foot

Plate 8. Six-Board Pine Chest

SIX-BOARD PINE CHEST

The six-board pine chest, although very plain, is a very interesting piece of furniture. It is called a six-board chest, because early chests made in this fashion were made of six wide pine boards. Twentieth-century cabinetmakers are not often lucky enough to be able to obtain boards of this width.

The chest is dovetailed together at each corner with wide dovetails. It is further fastened together with cut nails having battered heads. The lid is fastened to the chest with wooden hinges. These consist of two wooden cleats fastened to the top, and they swing on dowels driven into holes bored through the cleats and into the ends of the chest.

In shape, the feet resemble a turnip, and are therefore so named. They are fastened to the chest by means of split dowels, turned as part of the feet, having wedges driven in to spread them.

BILL OF MATERIAL

Top	1 pc.	1	x 26¼	x 57½
Front and back	2 pc.	⅞	x 19	x 54
Ends	2 pc.	⅞	x 19	x 25½
Bottom	1 pc.	⅞	x 24½	x 53
Feet	4 pc.	4	diam.	x 6
Hinges	2 pc.	1	x 2	x 25
Dowels	2 pc.	½	diam.	x 2 long

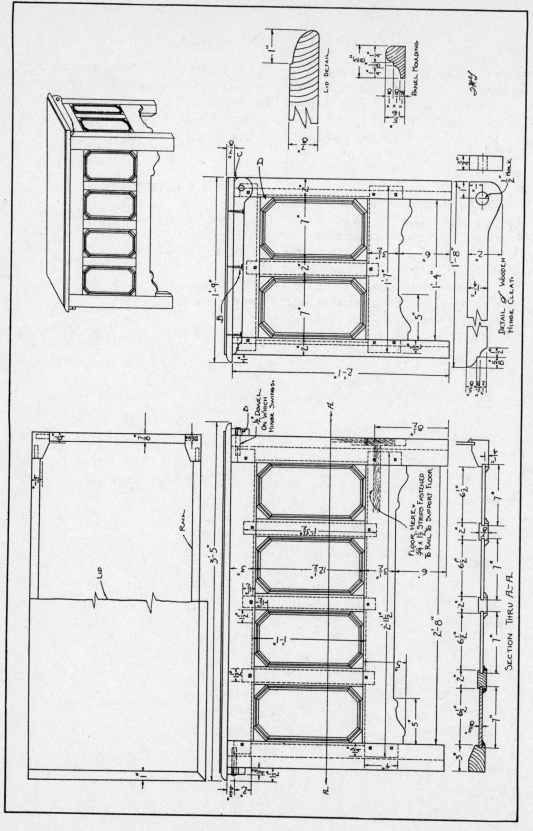

Plate 9. Paneled Chest

PANELED CHEST

Chests are very popular pieces of bed-room furniture. The design shown may be used to make a handsome cedar chest, al-though oak or maple would be more suit-able woods.

Paneled construction is good for chests, because it takes care of shrinkage and expansion caused by changing weather conditions. This is an important considera-tion, because the inside of a chest should not be stained or finished. If a good finish is put on the outside, the effects of heat and moisture will cause the inside to season much more quickly than the outside. If the wood is not well seasoned, the effects of this unequal drying often are disastrous. Paneled construction, because it allows ex-pansion and contraction in one piece with-out causing undue stress on other parts, is ideal. It is, therefore, a good construction to use where wide surfaces, like the sides of the chest, are necessary.

The construction is self-evident from a study of the drawing. The legs should be beveled on the inside as shown, thus cut-ting out sharp corners. To open the lid, wooden hinge cleats are swung on ½-inch dowels which should be made of straight-grained hickory. As shown at C, the upper edge of the back must be slightly rounded so the lid will have clearance enough when it is to be opened.

The small triangular blocks, D, which are ¼ inch thick, as well as the panel molding, are fastened with brads after the chest has been assembled.

BILL OF MATERIAL

Legs	4 pc. 2	x 3	x 25
Top	1 pc. ⅞ x 21		x 41
Upper rails, front and back frame	2 pc. ⅞ x 3		x 35½
Lower rails, front and back frame	2 pc. ⅞ x 5		x 35½
Upper rails, end frames	2 pc. ⅞ x 3		x 19
Lower rails, end frames	2 pc. ⅞ x 5		x 19
Stiles in all frames	8 pc. ⅞ x 2		x 15½
Panels, front and back frames	8 pc. ⅜ x 7		x 13
Panels, end frames	4 pc. ⅜ x 7½	x 13	
Hinge cleats	2 pc. ¾ x 2		x 20
Panel molding, approx. 45 feet			
Floor of chest	⅞ x 18¼ x 36¼		
48 small corner blocks	¼ x 1½ x 1½		
Floor strips	2 pc. ¾ x 1½ x 36¼		
Floor strips	2 pc. ¾ x 1½ x 16¾		

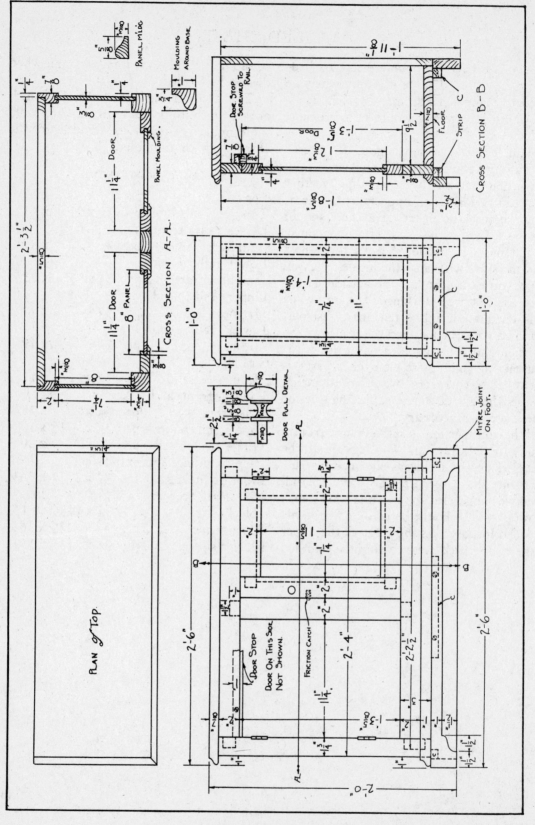

Plate 10. Small Two-Door Cabinet

SMALL TWO-DOOR CABINET

A small cabinet, like the one shown, is often just the thing needed under a window to hold books or magazines. It may serve as a window seat as well, and can be used to support a radio.

The cross-section views show the construction details clearly. Both ends and the doors are paneled. Since all panels are the same thickness, the construction work should be so arranged that all grooves meant to receive the panels may be cut at the same time. The vertical pieces on the back of each end are rabbeted so the back will fit flush with their edges.

The feet are mitered on the front corners. They should be assembled, and the strips C screwed to the inside upon which to rest the cabinet. After the feet have been fastened to the cabinet, the molding may be tacked on.

The doors should be made and fitted last. They are held in place by friction catches. If so desired, panel molding may be used on the doors as well as on the ends of the cabinet. This will greatly add to its beauty.

BILL OF MATERIAL

Top	1 pc.	$\frac{7}{8}$ x	12	x 30
Vertical corner pieces on front of cabinet	2 pc.	$1\frac{3}{4}$ x	$1\frac{3}{4}$ x	$20\frac{5}{8}$
Vertical corner pieces on rear of cabinet	2 pc.	$\frac{7}{8}$ x	2	x $20\frac{5}{8}$
Upper rail, under top	1 pc.	$\frac{7}{8}$ x	2	x $26\frac{1}{2}$
Lower rail, above base	1 pc.	$\frac{7}{8}$ x	3	x $26\frac{1}{2}$
Stile between doors	1 pc.	$\frac{7}{8}$ x	2	x $17\frac{5}{8}$
Upper end rails	2 pc.	$\frac{7}{8}$ x	2	x $9\frac{1}{4}$
Lower end rails	2 pc.	$\frac{7}{8}$ x	3	x $9\frac{1}{4}$
End panels	2 pc.	$\frac{3}{8}$ x	8	x $16\frac{3}{8}$
Front foot	1 pc.	$\frac{7}{8}$ x	$2\frac{1}{2}$ x	30
Back foot	1 pc.	$\frac{7}{8}$ x	$2\frac{1}{2}$ x	30
End feet	2 pc.	$\frac{7}{8}$ x	$2\frac{1}{2}$ x	12
Base molding			see drawing	
Back		$\frac{5}{8}$ x	$20\frac{5}{8}$ x	$27\frac{1}{2}$
Door stiles	4 pc.	$\frac{7}{8}$ x	2	x $15\frac{5}{8}$
Door rails	4 pc.	$\frac{7}{8}$ x	2	x $9\frac{1}{4}$
Door panels	2 pc.	$\frac{3}{8}$ x	8	x $12\frac{3}{8}$
Door pulls	2 pc.	$\frac{7}{8}$ diam. x	$2\frac{1}{2}$	
Panel molding.				

Fig. 6. Small Two-Door Cabinet

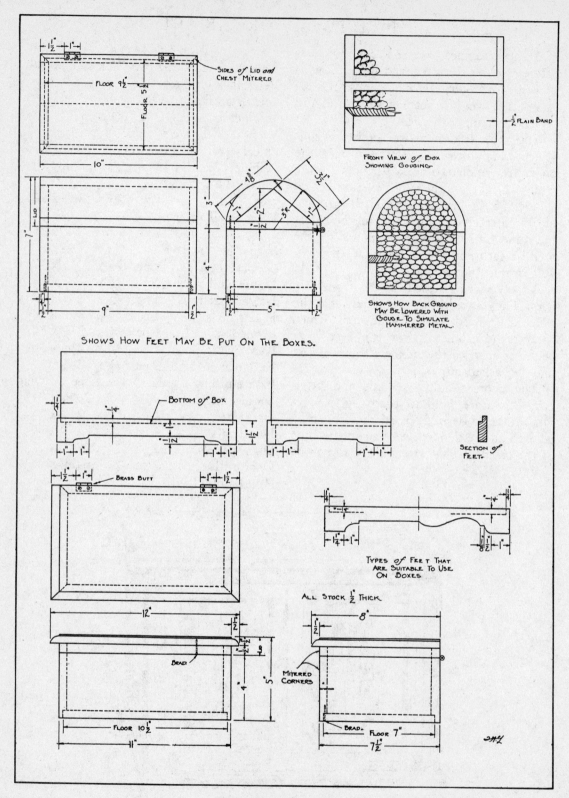

Plate 11. Two Small Boxes

SMALL BOXES

Both small boxes shown are simple to make and can be used as containers for gifts, such as candy, stationery, etc. They may be made with or without feet, as desired. Several suggestions for feet are given in the drawing. If feet are not added, it is advisable to glue a piece of felt to the bottom of the boxes to prevent their scratching furniture on which they are placed. The boxes are made as follows:

Round-Top Box: 1. Cut all stock, and square it to the sizes given in the cutting schedule.

2. Rabbet the bottom edges of the sides and ends to make a place for the floor.

3. Miter the corners, and assemble the box with brads and glue.

4. To make the lid, miter and assemble the sides and ends of the lid.

5. Fasten the triangular-shaped ends to this frame.

6. Fit the top boards, fastening the narrower one first. These should not be rounded until after the lid has been assembled.

7. With a compass, lay out the 3-inch arc on each end, and round the top with a plane.

Flat-Top Box: To make the box proper, proceed as with the other box. The molding on the lid may be cut by machine, or may be made by first lowering the edges on three sides to a depth of 1/16 inch and then rounding them with a block plane and fine-toothed rasp.

Both boxes may be lined with felt, glued on the inside with wood glue if so desired.

MATERIAL FOR ROUND-TOP BOX

Ends of box	2 pc.	½ x	4	x	6
Sides of box	2 pc.	½ x	4	x	10
Bottom of box	1 pc.	½ x	5½	x	9½
Side pieces on lid	2 pc.	½ x	½	x	10
End pieces on lid	2 pc.	½ x	½	x	6
Triangular pieces on end of lid	2 pc.	½ x	2	x	5
Top pieces before { shaping	1 pc. 1	x	3½	x	10
	1 pc. 1	x	4⅜	x	10
Feet, if desired	See drawing				

MATERIAL FOR FLAT-TOP BOX

Top board of lid	1 pc.	½ x	8	x	12
Sides of lid	2 pc.	½ x	½	x	11
Ends of lid	2 pc.	½ x	½	x	7½
Sides of box	2 pc.	½ x	4	x	11
Ends of box	2 pc.	½ x	4	x	7½
Floor of box	1 pc.	½ x	7	x	10½
Feet, if desired	See drawing				

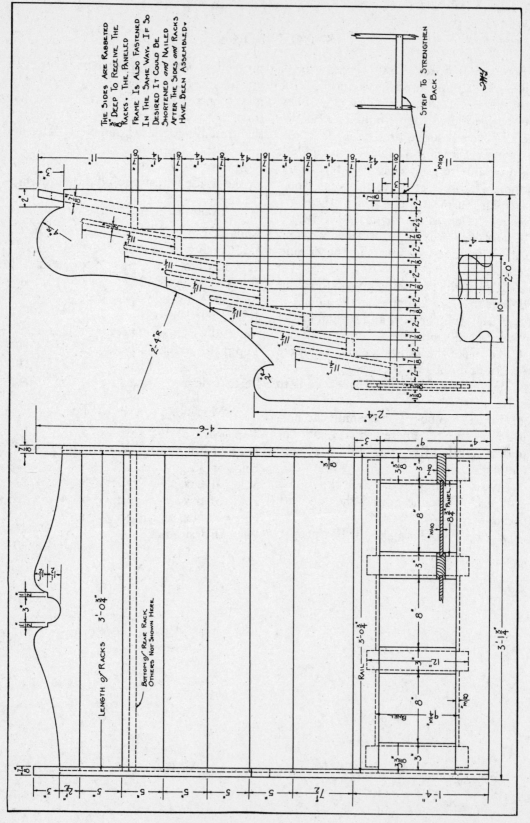

Plate 12. Magazine Rack

MAGAZINE RACK

One of the many things a school shop often is called upon to furnish is a magazine rack for the school library. The one shown here had its inspiration from a colonial settle. It is different from the conventional type of magazine rack usually found in school and public libraries, and is not very difficult to build.

The sides are first glued up, and then sawed on a band saw to the required shape. Grooves are then cut, into which to fit the back of each rack. The floors of the racks may be nailed to the wide boards after the entire piece has been assembled. The grooves are ⅜ inch deep and are cut with a router plane.

As suggested in the drawing, the paneled frame which forms the front of the case may be shortened ¾ inch, and merely butted against each side and nailed. To make the paneled frame, the rails and stiles first are cut to size. The edges of the stiles and one edge of each rail are then grooved, after which the mortises and tenons are cut and the frame is assembled.

The rack would be simpler to make if the back of each shelf were not inclined

at a slight angle. It will be found advisable, however, to make the shelves as shown, in order that the magazines may not lean forward and droop, thus making an unsightly appearance.

BILL OF MATERIAL

Sides _____2 pc. ⅞ x 24 x 54
W i d e boards in
 racks _____6 pc. ½ x 11¼ x 36¾
Scrolled top board__1 pc. ⅞ x 11¼ x 36¾
Floor boards for
 racks _____6 pc. ⅞ x 2¼ x 36
Floor board for up-
 per rack _____1 pc. ⅞ x 2¾ x 36
Upper rail of pan-
 eled frame _____1 pc. ⅞ x 3 x 36¾
Lower rail of pan-
 eled frame _____1 pc. ⅞ x 4 x 36¾
Outside stiles f o r
 paneled frame _____2 pc. ⅞ x 3⅜ x 12
Center stiles f o r
 paneled frame _____2 pc. ⅞ x 3 x 12
Panels _____3 pc. ⅜ x 8¾ x 9¾
Strip to strengthen
 back _____1 pc. ⅞ x 3 x 37¾

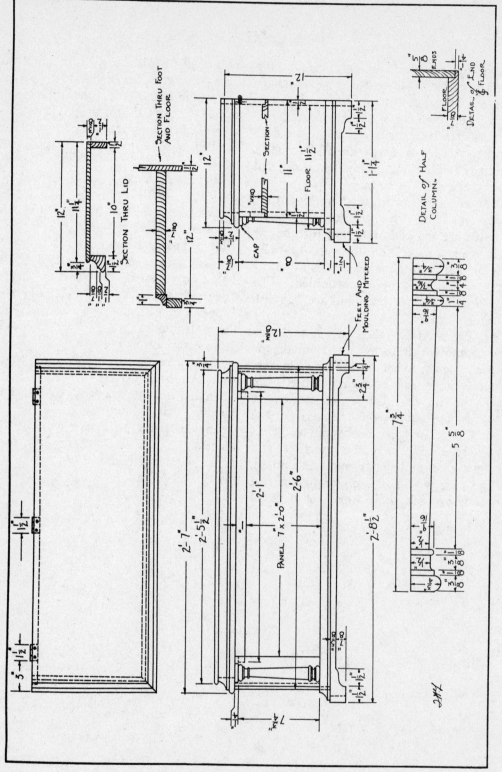

Plate 13. Bracket-Footed Radio Cabinet

BRACKET-FOOTED RADIO CABINET

It is rather incongruous to say that a radio cabinet is designed after the colonial manner, because radio is so modern. However, the spirit rather than the letter of colonial design has been aimed at.

The box of the cabinet should be made first. The ends of the box are rabbeted on both vertical edges for the front and back pieces to fit into them. A size has been given for the panel to be used. However, it will be possible to vary this size to a considerable extent by narrowing or widening the pieces back of the half columns and the top rail. The cabinet as designed is intended for a six-tube set.

The lid is built up of molding, mitered on the front corners, and a thin top board.

The hinge strip on the lid is fastened between the end moldings with butt joints.

The feet are made last of all and are assembled before being fastened to the cabinet. The column may be turned and then sawed in half.

BILL OF MATERIAL

Top of lid............1 pc. $\frac{3}{8}$ x $11\frac{1}{4}$ x $29\frac{1}{2}$
Molding for lid about 5 feet long
End boards ....2 pc. $\frac{5}{8}$ x 11 x 8
B o a r d s back of
  half columns ......2 pc. $\frac{1}{2}$ x $2\frac{3}{4}$ x 8
Front feet ....1 pc. $\frac{3}{4}$ x $1\frac{1}{2}$ x $32\frac{1}{2}$
Molding above feet, about 5 feet long
End feet................2 pc. $\frac{3}{4}$ x $1\frac{1}{2}$ x $13\frac{1}{4}$
Half c o l u m n s,
  split from 1 piece $1\frac{1}{2}$ diam. x $7\frac{3}{4}$
Back .... $\frac{1}{2}$ x 12 x $29\frac{1}{2}$
Floor ....1 pc. $\frac{7}{8}$ x $11\frac{1}{2}$ x 30

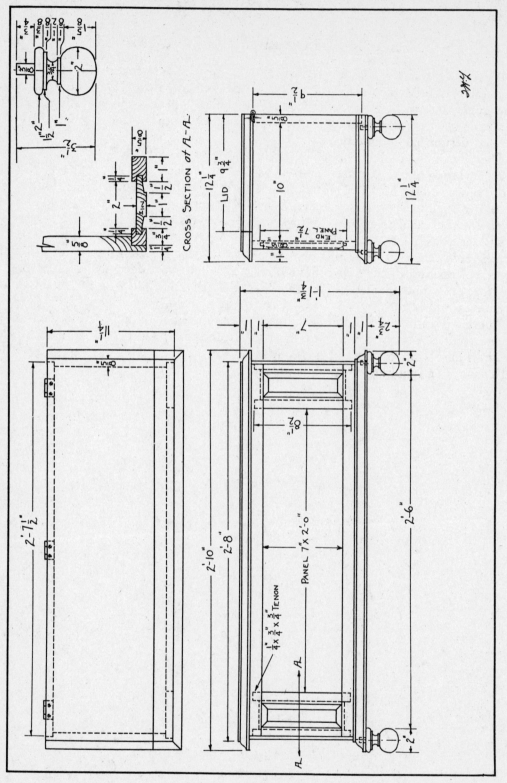

Plate 14. Ball-Footed Radio Cabinet

BALL-FOOTED RADIO CABINET

The construction of this cabinet is similar to the bracket-footed cabinet. The top, however, is made of a single board, which after being molded around three edges, is cut into two parts. The front piece is fastened permanently to the cabinet, while the rear part swings open on hinges.

The small, raised panels on each side of the front form an interesting decoration, and furnish a good problem in surface enrichment. These panels may be easily raised with a chisel.

The ball feet are fastened by means of dowels turned as part of the feet.

BILL OF MATERIAL

Top*	1 pc.	1 x 12¼ x 34
Ends	2 pc.	⅝ x 11¼ x 9
Upper and lower rails	2 pc.	⅝ x 1 x 31½
End stiles	2 pc.	⅝ x ¾ x 8½
Inside stiles	2 pc.	⅝ x 1 x 8½
Panels	2 pc.	½ x 2½ x 7½
Floor	1 pc.	1 x 12¼ x 34
Feet	4 pc.	2 diam. x 3½
Back		⅝ x 9½ x 31½

*Includes lid and crosspiece.

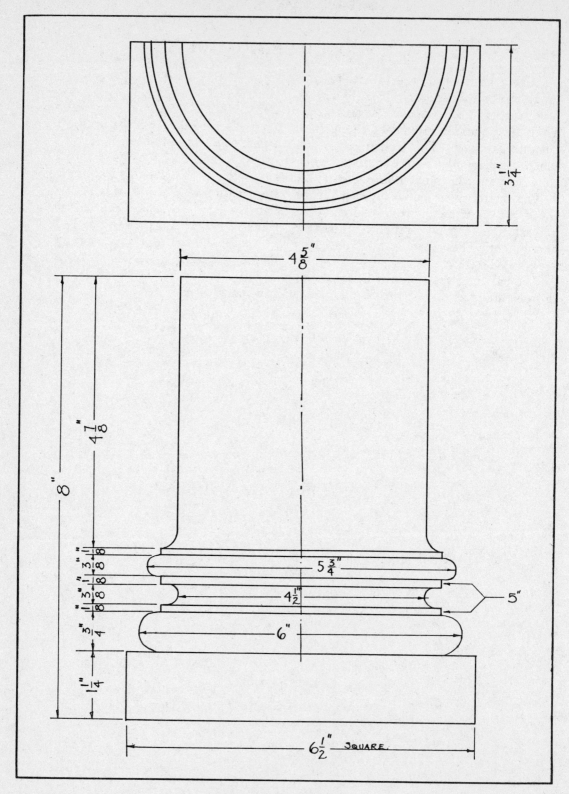

Plate 15. Turned Book Ends

TURNED BOOK ENDS

These book ends are classic in design, imitating the base of a Roman column. After having been turned, the block is split on the band saw, thus forming a pair of book ends. The square base may be fastened either before sawing or after, as desired. If they are made of boldly figured blocks of walnut or mahogany, they will be very attractive. They should be highly polished with rottenstone after finishing, to bring out the full beauty of the grain. To give them stability, it is well to bore several holes into the base of the book ends and pour in molten lead. The bottoms should be covered with green felt.

BILL OF MATERIAL

Base _____1 pc. 1¼ x 6½ x 6½
Column, to be split__1 pc. 6   diam. x 6¾

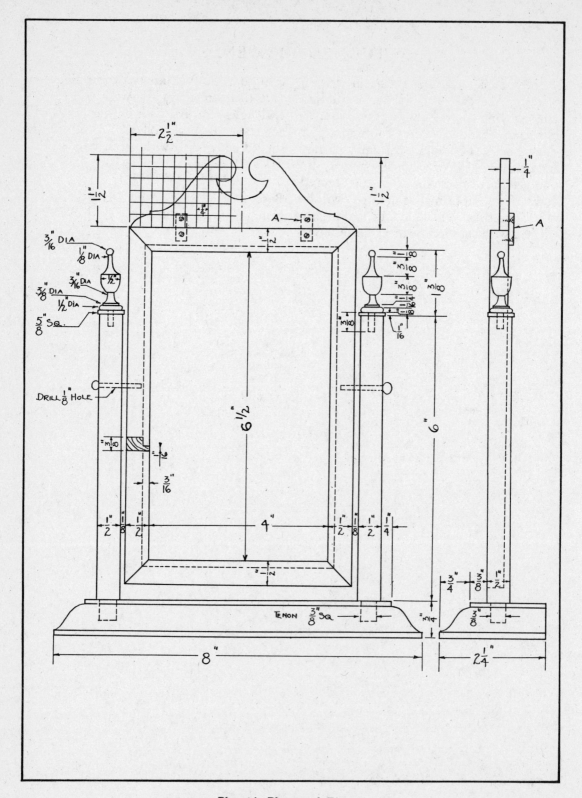

Plate 16. Photograph Frame

PHOTOGRAPH FRAME

Photograph frames usually are very popular projects. The one shown has been designed in the colonial spirit. The square posts on either side of the frame are mortised into the molded base, and are surmounted by two small turned finials.

The frame is allowed to swing on two pins of wood or brass. The scrolled top is fastened to the frame with small wooden or metal strips A and screws. A piece of felt is glued to the base of the frame.

BILL OF MATERIAL

Base	1 pc.	¾ x 2¼ x 8
Side posts	2 pc.	½ x ½ x 6½
Vertical pieces in frame	2 pc.	⅜ x ½ x 7½
Horizontal pieces in frame	2 pc.	⅜ x ½ x 5
Scroll top board	1 pc.	¼ x 1½ x 5
Urn finials	2 pc.	½ diam. x 1¾
Finial bases	2 pc.	1/16 x ⅝ x ⅝

Fig. 7. Photograph Frame

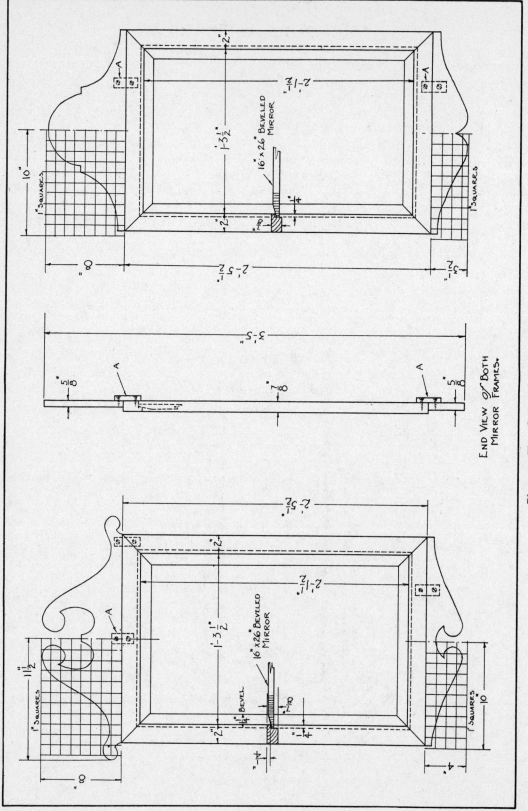

Plate 17. Two Colonial Mirror Frames

TWO COLONIAL MIRROR FRAMES

The two colonial mirror frames are very simple in design, and are made of the same-sized stock. If still further variety is desired in this project, the maker should be allowed to design a differently shaped scroll for the top or bottom. Certain types of molded frames also may be used.

The construction is self-evident when the drawings are examined. It might be well to use plywood for the scrolled pieces, but if well-seasoned wood is used, this is not necessary.

BILL OF MATERIAL
(Either mirror may be made from this stock)

Vertical molding _____ 2 pc. ⅞ x 2 x 29½
Horizontal molding ____ 2 pc. ⅞ x 2 x 19½
Scrolled top _____ 1 pc. ⅝ x 8 x 23
Scrolled bottom _____ 1 pc. ⅝ x 4 x 19½

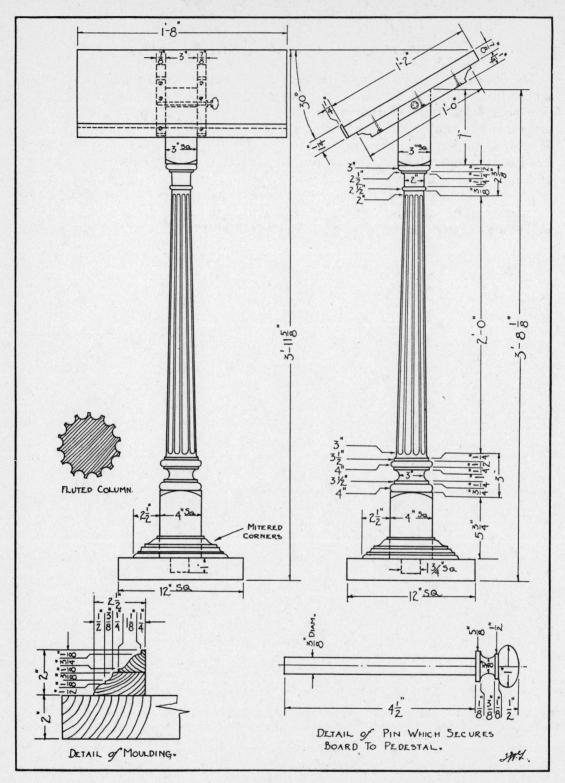

FLUTED COLUMN.

MITERED CORNERS

DETAIL OF MOULDING.

DETAIL OF PIN WHICH SECURES
BOARD TO PEDESTAL.

Plate 18. Lectern

LECTERN

A lectern like the one shown will be a handsome addition to the equipment of any hall where considerable public speaking or lecturing is done. The design may be somewhat modified and worked over into a music stand. For such use it will, of course, have to be made lower and lighter in weight. The construction of the piece is easily understood by examining the drawing.

The top is fastened to the pedestal by means of a wooden peg or pin which is passed through holes bored in the cleats and pedestal. Thus the top may be easily removed, since the pin is removable.

BILL OF MATERIAL

Base	1 pc. 2	x 12	x 12	
Column	1 pc. 4	x 4	x 43⅛	
Board	1 pc. ⅞	x 14	x 20	
Strip to hold book	1 pc. ¼	x 1¼	x 20	
Cleats	2 pc. ⅞	x 1¼	x 12	
Pin to hold top in place	1 pc. 1	diam.	x 5⅝	

Molding about 3 feet.

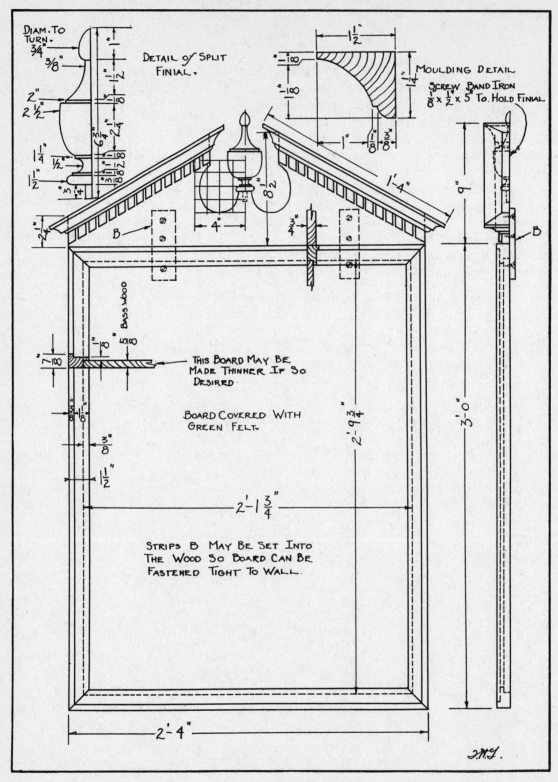

DIAM. TO TURN ¾"
³⁄₈"

DETAIL OF SPLIT FINIAL.

2"
2½"

1¼" ½
1½"

MOULDING DETAIL
SCREW BAND IRON
⅛ x ½ x 5 TO HOLD FINIAL

1'-4"

9"

B

B

BASS WOOD

THIS BOARD MAY BE MADE THINNER IF SO DESIRED.

BOARD COVERED WITH GREEN FELT.

⅜
1½"

2'-9¾"

3'-0"

2'-1¾"

STRIPS B MAY BE SET INTO THE WOOD SO BOARD CAN BE FASTENED TIGHT TO WALL.

2'-4"

Plate 19. Bulletin Board

BULLETIN BOARD

Schools, libraries, and commercial offices require bulletin boards. There is no reason why they should not be beautiful, since they usually are placed in a very conspicuous place. The one shown here is not merely a board with a frame around it, but is an attractive sign board, especially if painted white or ivory.

The frame may be made first. Then the pediment is made and fastened to the frame with either small strips of wood or, preferably, iron, as shown at B. The dentils are small blocks of wood about ¼ inch thick by ¾ inch wide and 1 inch long. They should be separated about ¼ inch from each other.

The finial, after having been turned on the lathe, must be cut flat on the back so it will not interfere with fastening the entire board against the wall.

BILL OF MATERIAL

Long pieces in
    frame _____2 pc. ⅞ x 1½ x 36
Short pieces in
    frame_____2 pc. ⅞ x 1½ x 28
Face board in pedi-
    ment _____1 pc. ¾ x 8½ x 28
Finial _____1 pc. 2½ diam. x 6¾
Molding about 36 inches long
Dentils, about ¼ thick x ¾ wide x 1 long
Board to be cov-
    ered with felt _____ ⅝ x 25¾ x 33¾

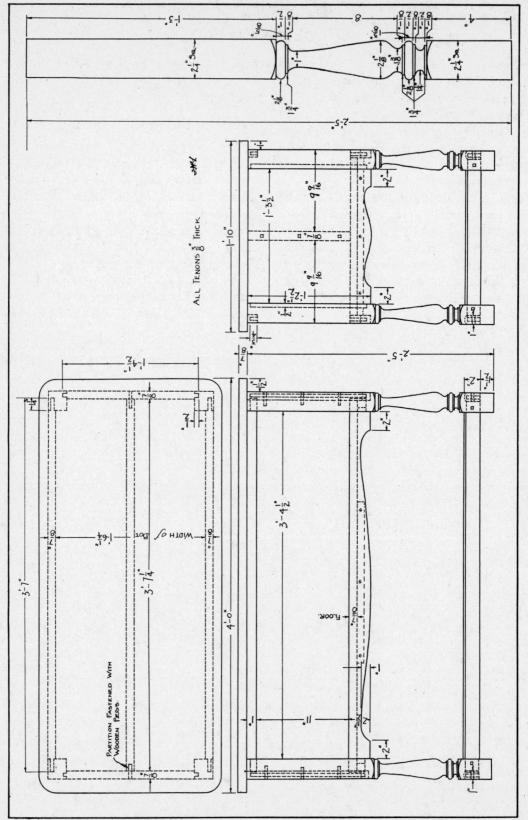

Plate 20. Bookcase Table or Encyclopedia Case

BOOKCASE TABLE OR ENCYCLOPEDIA CASE

This piece of furniture is very well adapted for use in a public library, a school, or in the home. When used to hold reference books, such as an encyclopedia, it is very handy, since a volume may be opened and perused on the large table surface. This saves time, especially when several volumes are to be examined.

This design may be modified so that the case can be placed against the wall, by making it single instead of double. To do this, the cabinet should be made only half the depth shown, and a back should be built in instead of the partition.

The apron and stretchers are fastened to the legs with mortise-and-tenon joints. These joints may be pinned and glued, or merely glued, as desired. The end boards are fastened to the legs by means of tongue-and groove joints. The partition is fastened in place before the top is fastened down.

BILL OF MATERIAL

Top _____1 pc. ⅞ x 22 x 48
Legs _____4 pc. 2¼ x 2¼ x 29
Ends _____2 pc. ⅞ x 16½ x 14½
Partition _____1 pc. ⅞ x 12 x 43¼
Lower aprons _____2 pc. ⅞ x 2½ x 43
Upper aprons _____2 pc. ⅞ x 1 x 43
Long stretchers ____2 pc. 1 x 2 x 43
Short stretchers ___2 pc. 1 x 2 x 18
Floor _____1 pc. ⅞ x 18¼ x 43¼
Cleats for bottom.

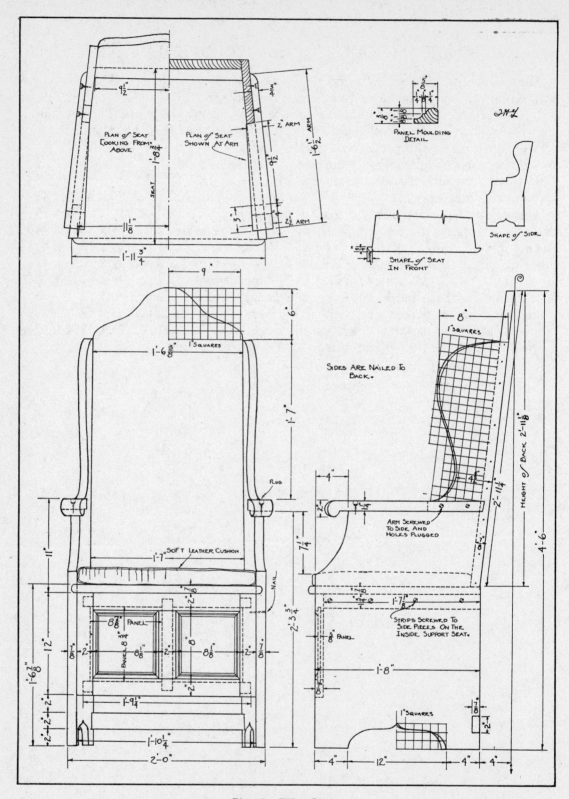

Plate 21. Wing Chair

WING CHAIR

We are told that wing chairs originally were made to keep drafts of cold air away from the heads of persons seated in them. Because the wing chair had a high back, it could be set near the fireplace, usually facing it, so that the occupant was protected from the cold on every side.

This wing chair may be made of pine or any other inexpensive wood, covered with tapestry or even cretonne, and painted or stained as desired. It makes an imposing seat for a public hallway or a semipublic meeting place.

The sides are glued up and then cut to shape on the band saw. The back is nailed between the two sides and ends at the seat.

The seat, the front of which is slightly rounded, is supported by the paneled front and by strips screwed to the sides on the inside. The arms are cut from a 2-inch plank and after being formed are fastened with wood screws. The screw heads are countersunk and the holes plugged.

The chair is fastened together with finishing nails, but it is well also to use glue where possible.

BILL OF MATERIAL

Sides	2 pc.	$\frac{7}{8}$ x 23 x 48
Back	1 pc.	$\frac{7}{8}$ x 19 x 35$\frac{1}{4}$
Seat	1 pc.	$\frac{7}{8}$ x 20$\frac{3}{4}$ x 23$\frac{3}{4}$
Arms	2 pc.	2 x 2$\frac{1}{2}$ x 18$\frac{1}{2}$
Paneled { Rails	2 pc.	$\frac{7}{8}$ x 2 x 21$\frac{1}{4}$
front { Stiles	3 pc.	$\frac{7}{8}$ x 2 x 12
{ Panels	2 pc.	$\frac{3}{8}$ x 8$\frac{3}{4}$ x 8$\frac{7}{8}$
{ Molding		
Back rail	1 pc.	$\frac{7}{8}$ x 2 x 20$\frac{3}{4}$
Strips to support seat	2 pc.	$\frac{7}{8}$ x 1$\frac{3}{4}$ x 19

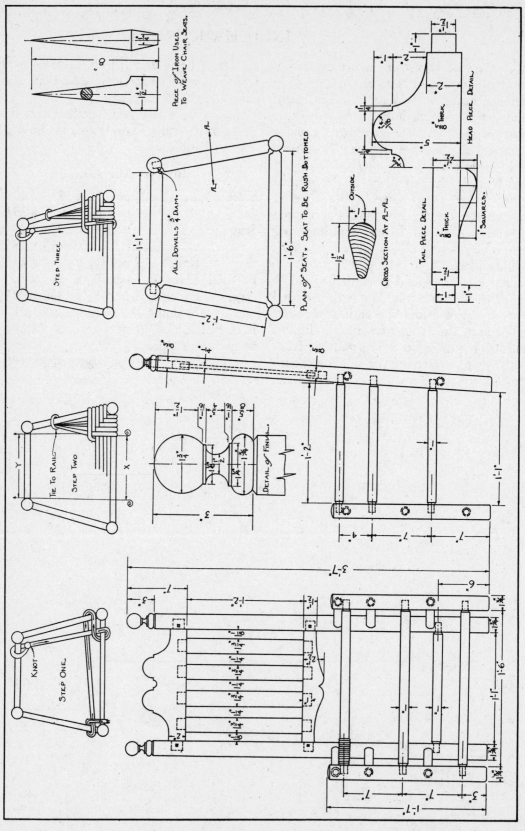

Plate 22. Bannister-Back Side Chair

BANNISTER-BACK SIDE CHAIR

One of the finest heritages the Pilgrim Century cabinetmakers gave us was their simple furniture. In some respects, it may have been severe or even crude, but it was always sturdy and often beautiful.

The first thing to consider in building the chair shown is, of course, the kind of wood to be used. Maple is recommended, with oak as second choice.

The first step in making the chair is to cut the stock to the required size and then turn all the pieces on the lathe. After this has been done, the holes should be bored. In order to bore them at the correct angle, the procedure is as follows: A heavy plank should be placed on the floor, and 1¾-inch holes bored into it in such a way that, when the legs are stuck into them, they will be the proper distance apart and also slant properly. A ¾-inch bit then should be placed in the brace and after the holes have been located on the legs they should be bored. This should be done by holding the brace in such a way that a center line running from the point of the bit to the head of the brace would, if extended, hit the center of each opposite hole.

The next step will be to make all mortises and tenons on the pieces that make up the back. After this has been done, the back is ready to be fitted and glued. Next, the front legs and their connecting stretchers should be glued together. After this has been done, the final step is to glue the stretchers that connect the back to the front legs. All the dowels can be turned on the ends of the stretchers with a hollow auger. The cross section of seat stretchers is shown at AA.

The proper finish to be used for this chair is an oil stain made up of about 2 ounces of burnt-umber color in boiled linseed oil and 1 pint of turpentine. The chair should be stained, and, after it has dried for at least 24 hours, given about 5 coats of orange shellac, sanding well between each coat. It then should be rubbed down with pumice stone and oil, followed with a coat of beeswax.

Beeswax is prepared in the following way: The wax is boiled down into hard cakes, and then broken up into small lumps. The lumps are then placed in a tin bucket, and enough turpentine is added to just cover the wax. After the wax has soaked up the turpentine, it is ready for use. A lump should then be folded in between cheesecloth, which should be rubbed over the piece, allowing the wax to penetrate as the cloth is rubbed back and forth.

On the same plate with the chair are illustrations showing how a rush seat is bottomed. In order to get a perfectly clear understanding of how this is done it is advisable for a beginner to study a book on the subject of chair seating. However, a few of the high points can be explained here. Genuine rush seats when carefully woven by an expert are very beautiful. The rushes should be cut and allowed to dry for a week or two in a barn loft or attic. They should then be soaked in water about 24 hours before using. The fibers also must be broken somewhat to make the rush pliable. This can be done by rolling them through an ordinary clothes wringer, a handful at a time. After this has been done, one end of several strands, according to the thickness of twist desired, should be tied to the back seat rung, as shown in step 1. Then, twisting the strands in a clockwise direction between the thumb and index finger, it should be brought over the front seat rung, around it and over itself, then over the right-side seat rung. From the bottom of this rung, it should be passed over the left-side seat rung, and so on. This is continued until the distance X,

Fig. 8. Bannister-Back Side Chair

same place on the rear seat rung and continuing as before, as shown in step 3. This causes the strands on one side to be parallel with those on the other side even though the sides of the seat are not parallel. By adding a new leaf of rush at regular intervals and twisting it in with the rest of the strand, an endless strand is the result. Each strand must be pushed as close to the adjacent one as possible, using the blunt end of the tool shown in the same plate. If in every round the end of a leaf is separated from the strand to be gathered up and twisted in with the adjacent strand, much strength will be added to the seat.

When the seat has been woven, it should be stuffed with scraps of the rush from the underside of the seat. These scraps should be forced in between the strands with a flat wooden paddle or stick. Several coats of shellac then should be applied to the seat before it has thoroughly dried.

BILL OF MATERIAL

Front legs ....2 pc. 1¾ diam. x 19
Back legs ....2 pc. 1¾ diam. x 43
Head piece ....1 pc. ⅝ x 5 x 15
Tail piece ....1 pc. ⅝ x 2½ x 15
Bannister slats ......4 pc. ¼ x 1¾ x 16
Front seat
   stretcher ....1 pc. 1 x 1½ x 20
Side seat
   stretchers ....2 pc. 1 x 1½ x 16
Back seat
   stretcher ....1 pc. 1 x 1½ x 15
Front stretchers ....2 pc. 1 diam. x 20
Lower side
   stretchers ....2 pc. 1 diam. x 15
Upper side
   stretchers ....2 pc. 1 diam. x 15½
Back stretcher ......1 pc. 1 diam. x 15

shown in step 2, equals the distance Y. When this point has been reached, all the strands going from front to back should be cut near the back seat rail and, after being gathered together, securely tied to the side seat rail as shown in step 2. The same thing should be done to the right and left sides. Then the same procedure should be begun as in step 1 by tying a strand to the

WALNUT LIBRARY TABLE

Although it is original in many respects, the design of this library table has been influenced very strongly by the work of Duncan Phyfe. Beauty of line and form are depended upon to make this table attractive, because it has no ornament of any kind, being without carving or molding.

The feet must be carefully made and joined to insure strength. They must be made of wood in which the grain as nearly follows the contour of the foot as possible. The section A-A shows how the feet and the block between them are joined. They are carefully mortised and tenoned together, glued and pinned.

Most of the outside surface of the connecting member is lowered to a depth of about $\frac{1}{8}$ inch, as shown in section E-E, leaving a raised border around it. This also is true of the twin face blocks B which are glued to the ends of the aprons. The surface is lowered with a router plane, and then carefully smoothed.

The drawer fronts are beaded around their edges, and the sides are blind dovetailed to these fronts. The drawers are kept from dropping down as they are pulled out, by the introduction of an upper run, as shown in the cross section at C-C. This piece also serves to help hold the top in place, screws being passed through it into the top from underneath.

In fastening the top, allowance is made for shrinkage, or any distortion whatsoever, by the simple method of boring holes through the pieces to which it is fastened, about three times the diameter of the screw, and then using iron washers to prevent the head of the screw from passing through the hole. These screws should be drawn only tight enough to hold the top securely in place, and not so tight as to cause the washer to sink into the wood. In this way, strains will never cause the top to come apart nor will the frame be strained in any way.

The isometric view shows the method of cutting the tenons on the aprons. This method should be used on both the back apron as well as on the rails above and below the drawers. This allows as much wood as possible on the outside walls of the mortise in the end aprons.

BILL OF MATERIAL

Top _____1 pc. $\frac{7}{8}$ x 24   x 47
Colonettes __4 pc. $1\frac{7}{8}$ largest diam. x $18\frac{1}{2}$

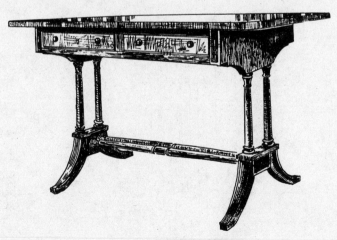

Fig. 9. Walnut Library Table

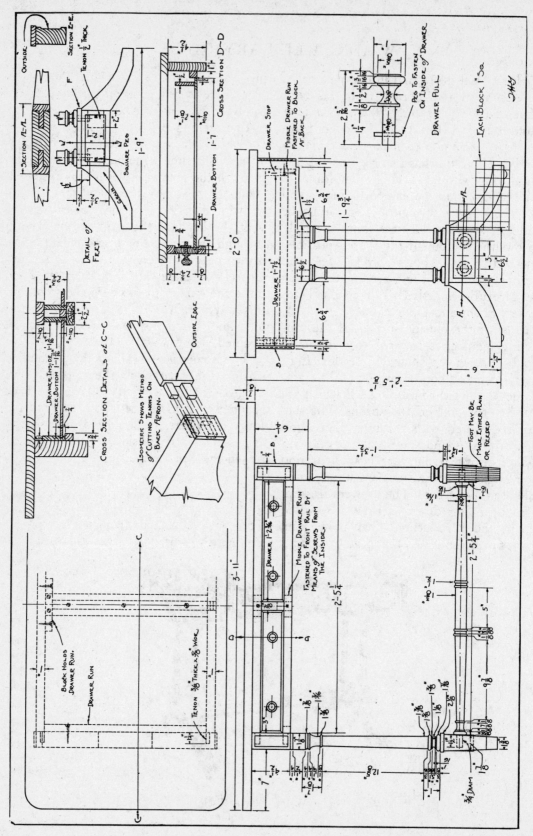

Plate 23. Walnut Library Table

Back apron*	1 pc.	1 x	4½ x	31¾
Top rail over drawers	1 pc.	1 x	⅞ x	31¾
Bottom rail under drawers	1 pc.	1 x	⅞ x	31¾
Stile between drawers	1 pc.	1 x	⅞ x	4½
End aprons under top	2 pc.	1⅞ x	6¼ x	21¾
Small applied blocks (B)	4 pc.	¼ x	1⅞ x	4½
Stretchers	2 pc.	1½ largest diam. x		32¼
Rectangular block immediately under colonettes, see (F)	2 pc.	½ x	2⅛ x	7
Blocks to which feet are joined	2 pc.	1⅞ x	3½ x	6½

Feet**	4 pc.	1⅞ x	4 x	12
Drawer fronts	2 pc.	¾ x	2¾ x	14 3/16
Drawer sides, pine or poplar	4 pc.	½ x	2¾ x	19¼
Drawer backs	2 pc.	½ x	2⅛ x	13 11/16
Drawer bottoms	2 pc.	⅜ x	13 11/16 x	19
Outside drawer runs	2 pc.	¾ x	⅞ x	19½
Middle drawer runs upper and lower	2 pc.	⅞ x	2½ x	19½
Guide between drawers	1 pc.	⅞ x	⅞ x	18½

*This includes length of tenons.
**Approx. size of stock.

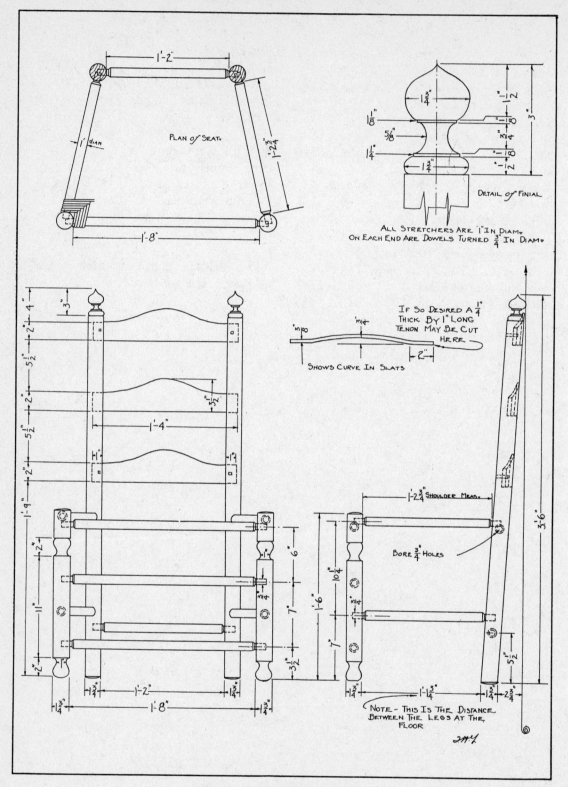

Plate 24. Ladder-Back Side Chair

LADDER-BACK SIDE CHAIR

This is a very simple and handsome chair that any craftsman or student, who has had a course in elementary turning, can make.

To assemble this chair, the same procedure should be followed as in making the Bannister-Back Side Chair. The slats may be cut from a 1-inch board on the band saw and smoothed with an adjustable curve plane and sandpaper.

It is the practice in furniture factories to scratch rings on the legs to indicate the places where holes are to be bored for stretchers. This is done on the lathe with the point of the skew chisel.

When the chair has been assembled, the seat should be rush bottomed, according to directions given for the Bannister-Back Side Chair. The author has bottomed several chairs with art fiber, which very closely resembles rush. It makes a seat that is very durable and handsome. Genuine rush seating, however, is more beautiful and probably more durable if done by an expert.

BILL OF MATERIAL

Front legs	2 pc.	1¾ diam.	x 18
Back legs	2 pc.	1¾ diam.	x 42
Slats*	3 pc.	1	x 3½ x 16
Side top seat stretchers	2 pc.	1 diam.	x 16¾
Lower side stretchers	2 pc.	1 diam.	x 16¼
Back stretchers	2 pc.	1 diam.	x 16
Front stretchers	3 pc.	1 diam.	x 22

*Size of stock from which to cut.

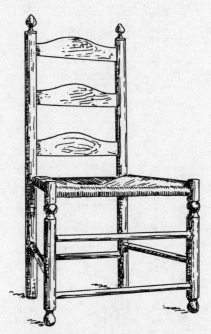

Fig. 10. Ladder-Back Side Chair

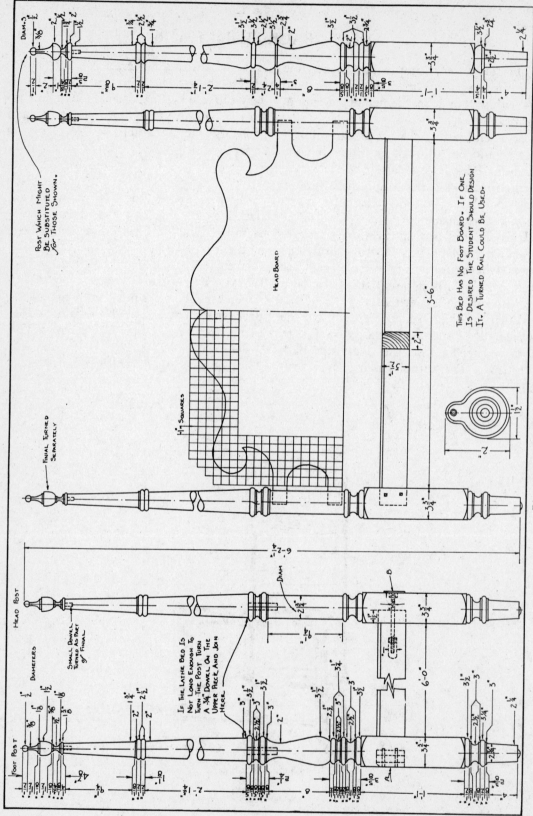

Plate 25. High-Post, Four-Poster Bed

HIGH-POST, FOUR-POSTER BED

Although this bed is a high-poster, it is not too high to look well in a medium-sized room. It is wide enough for two persons, but it does not take up an excessive amount of space. The width, of course, can easily be varied.

The bed has no footboard. It is suggested that the student be allowed to design one if one is desired. The foot rail and head rail are mortised into, and fastened permanently to, the posts with glue and wooden pins, as shown at A. They also come flush with the outside of the post. The side rails are necessarily removable, and are fastened with bed bolts, as shown at B. They may be bought in any length at a hardware store. The holes can be covered with bed-bolt covers of dull brass. The design of one is shown in the illustration.

If the bed of the lathe is not long enough to turn the bed posts to the full length, they may be turned up in two pieces and fastened together as shown in the illustration. The small finials at the top of the posts must be turned separately, since they are too delicate to be turned as a part of the post. Mahogany, maple, walnut, birch, or cherry are good woods to use in making this bed.

A box spring and a mattress should be used on this bed. Both may be bought in various sizes.

BILL OF MATERIAL

Posts	4 pc.	$3\frac{3}{4}$ x $3\frac{3}{4}$ x $69\frac{3}{8}$
Finials	4 pc.	$1\frac{1}{2}$ diam. x $5\frac{1}{2}$
Headboard	1 pc.	$\frac{7}{8}$ x 19 x 46
Head and foot rails	2 pc.	2 x $3\frac{1}{2}$ x 46
Side rails	2 pc.	2 x $3\frac{1}{2}$ x 76

Fig. 11. High-Post, Four-Poster Bed

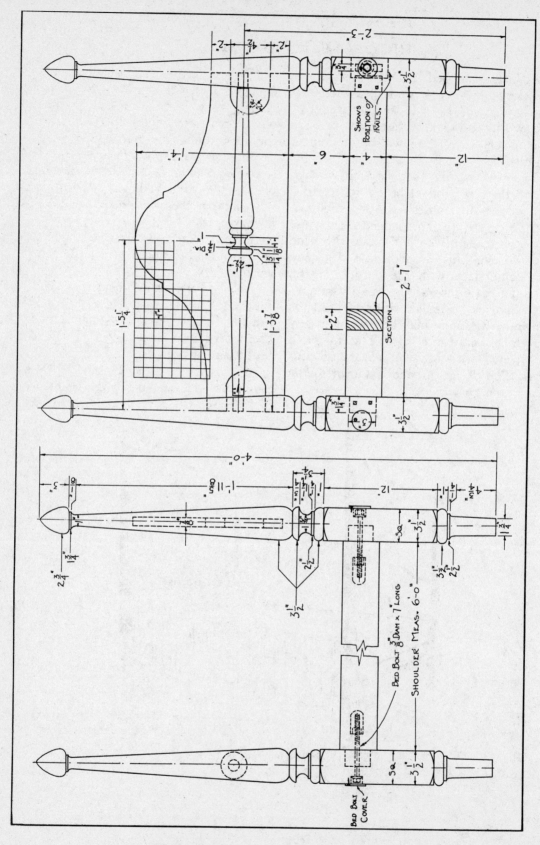

Plate 26. Low-Post Twin Bed

LOW-POST TWIN BED

The construction of this bed is practically the same as the high-post bed. Many people prefer low posts to high posts.

This bed has a foot rail. As in the case of the high-post bed, the headboard and rail, as well as both foot rails, are permanently fastened with mortise-and-tenon joints. The side rails are removable, being fastened with bed bolts which may be bought at a hardware store. The same type of bed-bolt covers are used to hide the holes as in the high-post bed. See the detail in the drawing of the high-post bed.

BILL OF MATERIAL

Posts	4 pc.	3½ x 3½ x 48
Headboard	1 pc.	⅞ x 16 x 34½
Turned stretcher	1 pc.	2½ diam. x 34½
Short rails	2 pc.	2 x 4 x 34½
Long rails	2 pc.	2 x 4 x 75½

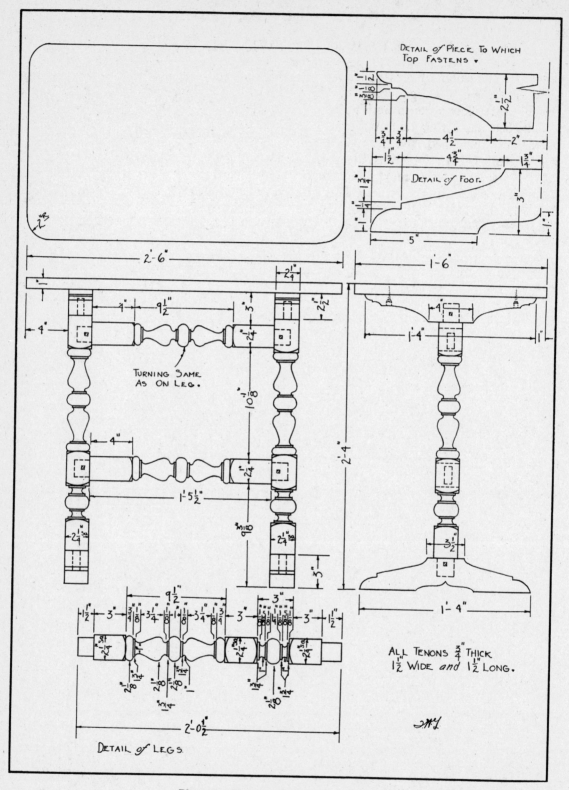

Plate 27. Small, Turned Trestle Table

SMALL, TURNED TRESTLE TABLE

The small, turned trestle table is suitable for a great many purposes, such as an end table for a sofa, a card table, or a bedside table.

The construction is very simple. After the legs and stretchers have been turned, they are fastened together with mortise-and-tenon joints. Holes may be bored for pins, and the pins driven in before the clamps are removed.

First, the legs and stretchers are glued together. Then they are scraped and sanded at the joints before the feet and upper crosspieces are fastened to them. When all members have been assembled and the joints dressed, the top is fastened with wood screws, set deep enough to allow the holes to be plugged so they will not show.

BILL OF MATERIAL

Legs	2 pc. 2¼ x 2¼ x 24½
Stretchers	2 pc. 2¼ x 2¼ x 20½
Feet	2 pc. 2¼ x 3 x 16
Crosspieces under top	2 pc. 2¼ x 2½ x 16
Top	1 pc. 1 x 18 x 30

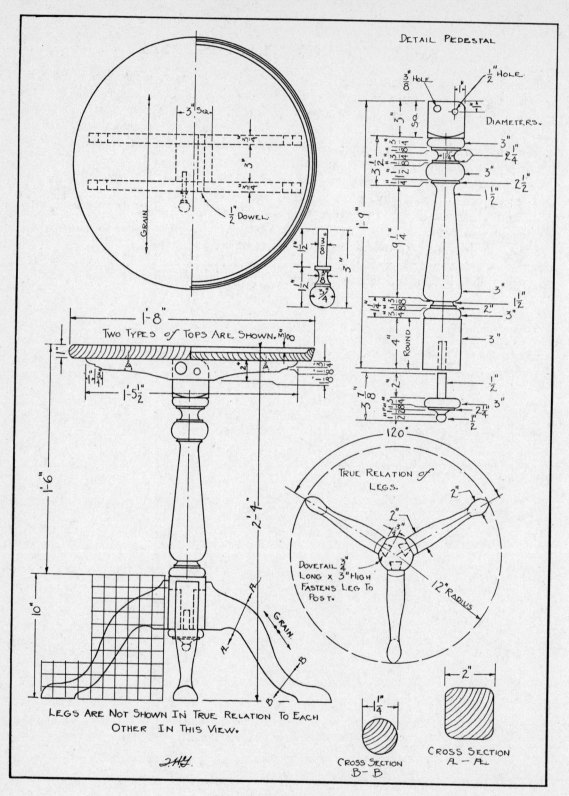

Plate 28. Tilt-Top Table

TILT-TOP TABLE

Tilt-top tables are very convenient when serving tea or coffee, and oftentimes also are very decorative pieces of furniture. Although the one shown is very plain, it has beautiful lines that make it attractive.

Two types of tops are shown. One is the plain, flat top with the slightly rounded edge; the other is one in which the surface has been lowered, leaving a border molding. If the latter top is made, it should be turned on a lathe. Most lathes are equipped with a faceplate on the headstock, having screw holes by means of which a top such as this one may be fastened and turned.

The top may be swung to a vertical position when the table is not being used and it is placed against the wall. The ½-inch dowel acts as a hinge. The top of the pedestal is rounded on one edge to give clearance enough to swing the table top.

After the pedestal has been turned, three flat surfaces are cut on it at the base where the feet are joined to it. The drop finial is fastened to it by means of a dowel turned as part of the finial.

The feet may be formed either as shown, or, if a simpler method of making them is desired, they may be cut from a 1-inch board, merely using the profile of the foot as a pattern. In either case they should be fastened to the pedestal with long dovetail joints, as shown in the drawing. Great care must be exercised in making these joints so they will fit perfectly.

BILL OF MATERIAL

Top	1 pc. 1	x 20	diam.
Pedestal	1 pc. 3	x 3	x 21
Cleats under top	2 pc. ¾	x 2	x 17½
Feet*	3 pc. 2	x 5	x 14½
Drop finial	1 pc. 3	diam.	x 3⅞
Peg to hold top	¾	diam.	x 3
Dowel	½	diam.	x 4½

*Stock from which to cut.

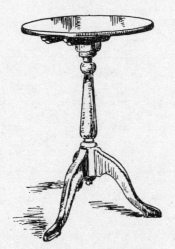

Fig. 12. Tilt-Top Table

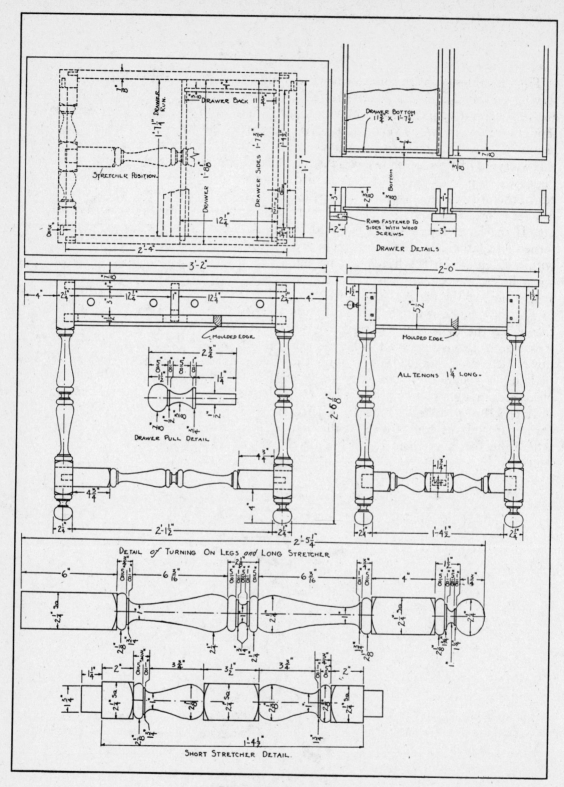

Plate 29. Tavern Table

TAVERN TABLE

Tavern tables were so named because this type of table was used in the taprooms of old wayside taverns on which to serve drinks and food. They are handy little tables for various purposes.

The turning on the legs and stretchers is practically alike. This duplication of turning for different members of the same piece of furniture is one of the basic principles of early American design. All rails and stretchers are fastened together with mortise-and-tenon joints. The long stretcher is fastened to the middle of the short-end stretchers.

The table is shown with two drawers. It may be very much simplified if only one or no drawer is used, and the feet may be left square instead of being turned.

BILL OF MATERIAL

Top	1 pc.	$\frac{7}{8}$ x 24		x 38
Legs	4 pc.	$2\frac{1}{4}$ x	$2\frac{1}{4}$ x	$29\frac{1}{4}$
Long stretcher	1 pc.	$2\frac{1}{4}$ x	$2\frac{1}{4}$ x	28
Short stretchers	2 pc.	$2\frac{1}{4}$ x	$2\frac{1}{4}$ x	19
Drawer fronts	2 pc.	$\frac{7}{8}$ x	3 x	$12\frac{1}{4}$
Drawer sides	4 pc.	$\frac{1}{2}$ x	3 x	$19\frac{3}{4}$
Drawer bottoms	2 pc.	$\frac{3}{8}$ x	$11\frac{3}{4}$ x	$19\frac{1}{2}$
Drawer backs	2 pc.	$\frac{3}{8}$ x	$2\frac{3}{8}$ x	$11\frac{3}{4}$
Outside drawer runs	2 pc.	$\frac{7}{8}$ x	2 x	$19\frac{1}{4}$
	2 pc.	$\frac{3}{4}$ x	$1\frac{3}{8}$ x	$16\frac{1}{2}$
Center drawer runs	1 pc.	$\frac{7}{8}$ x	3 x	$19\frac{1}{4}$
	1 pc.	$\frac{3}{4}$ x	1 x	$19\frac{1}{4}$
Drawer pulls	4 pc.	$\frac{7}{8}$ diam. x	$2\frac{3}{4}$	
Back apron	1 pc.	$\frac{7}{8}$ x	$5\frac{1}{2}$ x	28
Side aprons	2 pc.	$\frac{7}{8}$ x	$5\frac{1}{2}$ x	19
Front drawer rail	1 pc.	$\frac{7}{8}$ x	$1\frac{1}{2}$ x	28

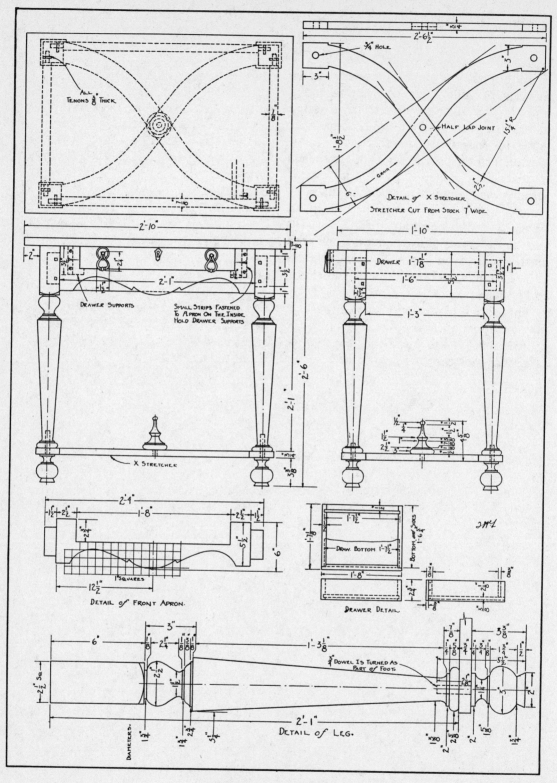

Plate 30. Lowboy Table

LOWBOY TABLE

The lowboy table is in reality a simple lowboy. Lowboys were much prized in colonial days, not only because of their beauty but also for their varied usefulness. The lowboy was used as a dressing table in milady's boudoir, or as a small serving table in the dining room, and was ofttimes placed in a hallway under a mirror. Many lowboys were made in the William-and-Mary style as is this one, with the trumpet- or vase-shaped legs and crossed stretchers. The design of the one shown has been simplified as much as possible to make it a practical project for the home workshop or for school-shop construction.

The aprons are joined to the legs with mortise-and-tenon joints, and the joints are made flush on the outside. To obtain maximum strength, square wooden pegs should be driven through the leg, into the tenon, besides gluing. The X stretchers are joined where they cross by half lapping both stretchers. After the stretchers have been joined together, holes are bored to fasten the finial and feet. Dowels on these should be turned as part of the feet and finial. The dowels on the feet are turned long enough so they may be passed through the X stretcher into the legs and glued, thus making a permanent joint. The drawers may be dovetailed or merely nailed. The former type of construction is the best and most desirable.

Bill of Material

Legs	4 pc. 3¼ diam. x 25	
Feet	4 pc. 3 diam. x 5½	
Top	1 pc. ⅞ x 22 x 34	
Front apron	1 pc. ⅞ x 6 x 28	
Back apron	1 pc. ⅞ x 5½ x 28	
End aprons	2 pc. ⅞ x 5½ x 18	
Drawer front	1 pc. ⅞ x 2¾ x 20	
X stretchers*	2 pc. ¾ x 7 x 38	
Finial	1 pc. 3 diam. x 4⅝	
Drawer sides	2 pc. ½ x 2¾ x 18¾	
Drawer bottom	⅜ x 18¾ x 19½	
Drawer back	1 pc. ⅜ x 2⅛ x 19½	
Drawer supports	2 pc. 1½ x 3½ x 18¼	

*Stock from which to cut.

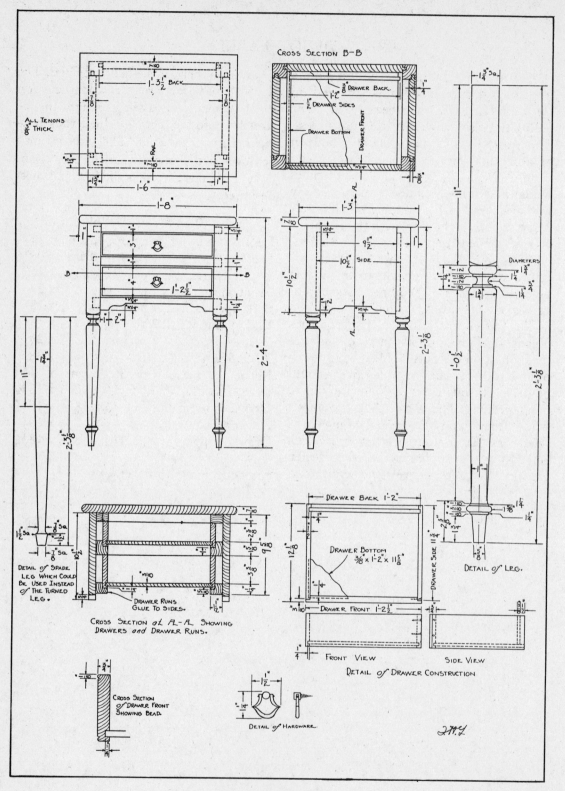

Plate 31. Sewing Table

SEWING TABLE

The little sewing table shown here illustrates very nicely how careful designing will beautify even the simplest piece of furniture. This table is an interesting problem, and the finished piece will do credit to any home.

The top is very plain, being merely rounded slightly on all edges.

It may be fastened to the frame by means of screws from beneath, or with table-top fasteners.

Two kinds of legs are shown. The turned legs are simple and well shaped. If square legs are desired instead, the spade-footed leg shown is very well suited to the design.

The construction is simple. The back and sides are jointed to the legs by means of ½-inch tongue-and-groove joints. The rails and apron in front are fastened with mortise-and-tenon joints. As will be noticed in the plan view, all joints are made flush on the outside.

The drawers are made with simple nailed joints. If the maker has the time and experience necessary, dovetail joints should be used. The design for the hardware is, of course, only a suggestion, since there are many other designs that may be used. Care should be taken, however, not to choose too ornate a pull for this table.

BILL OF MATERIAL

Legs	4 pc.	1¾ x 1¾ x 27⅛
Top	1 pc.	⅞ x 15 x 20
End boards	2 pc.	⅞ x 10½ x 10½
Rails above drawers	2 pc.	⅞ x 1 x 16½
Rail under lower drawer	1 pc.	⅞ x 1½ x 16½
Upper drawer front	1 pc.	¾ x 3 x 14½
Lower drawer front	1 pc.	¾ x 4 x 14½
Upper drawer sides	2 pc.	½ x 3 x 11¾
Lower drawer sides	2 pc.	½ x 4 x 11¾
Drawer bottoms	2 pc.	⅜ x 11⅝ x 14
Upper drawer back	1 pc.	⅜ x 2⅜ x 14
Lower drawer back	1 pc.	⅜ x 3⅜ x 14
Drawer runs		See drawing
Back board	1 pc.	⅞ x 10½ x 15½

Fig. 13. Sewing Table

FOUR-GATE GATE-LEG TABLE

One of the most handsome of all styles of Early American tables was the gate-leg table. It was, and still is, a particularly fine table to use as a dining table because it has all the qualities that a good dining table should possess with possibly one exception. The exception is that, for the person seated at the end of the center board, the bracing at the bottom of the legs is likely to interfere somewhat with comfortable sitting. However, if the person seated there will put his feet inside the cross stretcher, no discomfort will be experienced. In all other respects these tables are a fine example of what seventeenth-century artisans could do.

It will be found, if a study is made of gate-leg tables, that a certain conventional form was used in all the turnings. From this, no good example deviated very much. This is true not only of the gate-leg tables but of the butterfly tables, of the turned-leg tilt-top tables, and many others as well. Turning imposes certain limitations, and when a beautiful form was discovered, it was widely copied with very few variations.

The table here presented has four gates. Two are on each side of the table, and offer adequate support for each leaf. Notice that the hinges used to swing the leaves are longer on one side of the barrel than on the other. These are the proper kind of hinges to use, because they must be fastened with the barrel directly below the top edge of the leaf joint. This necessitates a longer leaf on one side of the barrel than the other.

The table contains a drawer in one end. The original purpose of this drawer was, of course, to hold the silver used at meal-times.

The drawer sides are extended beyond the rear of the drawer so that it may be pulled out for its entire length and still be supported on the drawer runs and drawer guides.

The gates, when closed, fold into the frame in such a way that they do not interfere with the leaf as it hangs in a vertical position. This is accomplished by cutting away part of the top of the leg and also a part of the apron on the table, as shown at D.

The table top, which is oval in shape, is laid out by most cabinetmakers with the trammel, also called an "ellipsograph." However, the method of laying it out shown in the drawing, if carefully done, is very satisfactory.

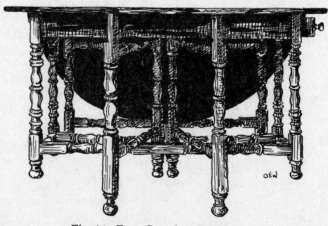

Fig. 14. Four-Gate Gate-Leg Table

BILL OF MATERIAL

Top leaves .... 2 pc. 7/8 x 19½ x 45
Top center .... 1 pc. 7/8 x 21   x 48
8 legs .... 8 pc. 2   x 2   x 29½
Short legs on
gates .... 4 pc. 2   x 2   x 17¾
Crosspieces on
gates .... 8 pc. 2   x 2   x 14
Long stretchers
on each side of
table .... 2 pc. 2   x 2   x 37
Short stretchers
on end of table ... 2 pc. 2   x 2   x 17
Long aprons .... 2 pc. 1¼ x 5½ x 37
Short apron on end
of table .... 1 pc. 7/8 x 6   x 17

Stretcher over
drawer .... 1 pc. 1   x 1   x 17
Stretcher under
drawer .... 1 pc. 1   x 1½ x 17
Drawer front .... 1 pc. 1   x 3½ x 15
Drawer sides .... 2 pc. ½ x 3½ x 34
Drawer bottom .... 1 pc. 3/8 x 14   x 22⅜
Drawer back .... 1 pc. 3/8 x 2⅞ x 14
Feet under short
legs of gate .... 4 pc. 2   x 2   x 7¾
Drawer runs .... 2 pc. 1½ x 1½ x 35
Drawer stop .... 1 pc. 1   x 1   x 16½
Upper drawer
guides .... 2 pc. 1   x 1½ x 35
Spacer for drawer
sides .... 1 pc. 3/8 x 3½ x 14

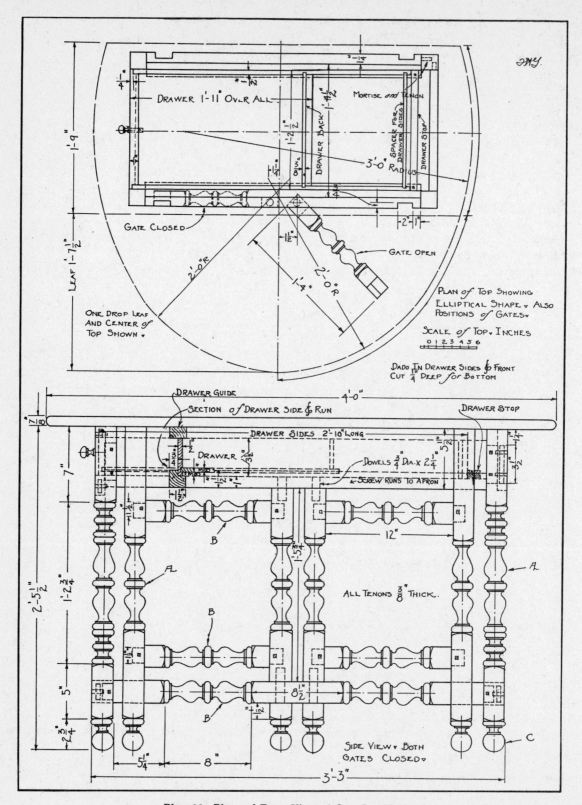

Plate 32. Plan and Front View of Gate-Leg Table

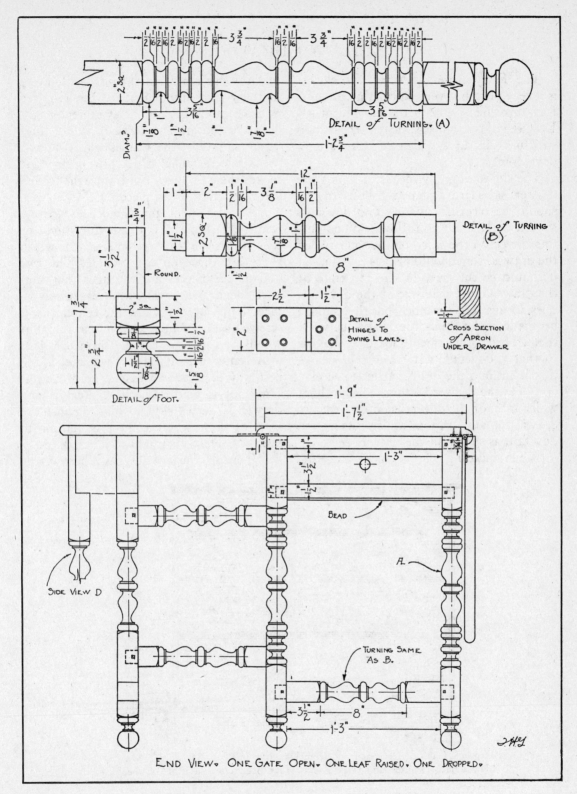

DETAIL OF TURNING. (A)

DETAIL OF TURNING (B)

ROUND.

DETAIL OF FOOT.

DETAIL OF HINGES TO SWING LEAVES.

CROSS SECTION OF APRON UNDER DRAWER

BEAD

SIDE VIEW D

A

TURNING SAME AS B.

END VIEW. ONE GATE OPEN. ONE LEAF RAISED. ONE DROPPED.

Plate 33. End View and Stretchers of Gate-Leg Table

CHEST OF DRAWERS

The Early American chest of drawers is a very plain but very fascinating piece of furniture. Being plain, it is easy to make. Despite its apparent simplicity it has certain structural features which require care in developing.

The dovetailing, by means of which the drawer sides are fastened to the fronts, should be carefully made. The dovetails should be laid out as follows: When cutting dovetails, the wood on the top edge of the drawer front should always remain, but it should be cut away on the top edge of the drawer sides. The size of the dovetails does not matter very much, but they should be made wider than the spaces between them. Their arrangement should be planned so that a dovetail will cover the groove that is cut into the drawer front to receive and hold the drawer bottom. The angle at which most of the dovetails on early drawers was cut is 11 degrees, which cuts a good dovetail, as shown in the drawing.

When building the chest of drawers, first the ends and top should be glued up in the rough and planed to the required thickness after gluing. After the ends have been dressed and cut to size, dadoes must be cut to receive the frames which support the drawers. This type of construction makes the chest very rigid, since the frames are glued to the end pieces.

To make the frames, mortises are cut into the back and front rails to receive the tenons cut on the crosspieces, of which there are three on each frame. The two outside crosspieces are the ones that support the drawer, while the central crosspiece is the one to which the center run is screwed. The center run is the strip of wood marked D in the sketch in detail A.

A center run, if carefully made, is the best way to insure an easy-sliding drawer. Unless it is guided in the center, a long drawer is very likely to bind against the sides of the case, since there is nothing to keep it perfectly straight in its track.

When all the frames have been made

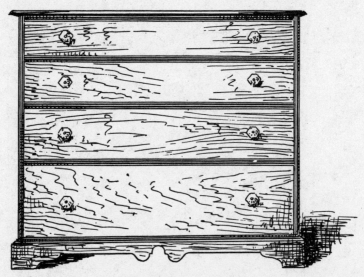

Fig. 15. Chest of Drawers made from Drawings in Plates 34 and 35. The Locks Have Been Omitted and Glass Knobs Have Been Used in Place of the Metal Pulls

and assembled, and when they have been glued to the ends of the chest, the feet should be made. These consist of four pieces joined on the front corners by splined miter joints. The back piece is gained into the end pieces in the same way as the back of the chest is gained into the end pieces. The feet may be laid out and cut on the band saw. After assembling them, strips should be glued and screwed to the inside faces, as shown at **B**. These strips support the chest, and by means of them the chest is fastened to the feet.

Next, three edges of the top should be molded and the top then fastened down by means of screws to the crosspieces and rails of the upper frame. When the top has been put in place, the back may be nailed on. It is best to nail the boards to the back horizontally with finishing nails.

The drawers should be made and fitted last of all. Their construction already has been partly explained. Note that the drawer backs are fitted last, into dadoes cut into the sides. Because the drawer bottom is likely to shrink, it is advisable not to fasten it to the back. It should be fastened to the sides only enough to keep it in place. The grooves in the sides and front of the drawer are about ¼ inch deep.

When completed, the chest of drawers should be well sanded and smoothed. Varnish should be used as a protecting coat. The inside as well as the outside of the chest should have at least one coat of varnish as a protection against checking or splitting, due to unequal drying.

Bill of Material

Wood: oak, maple, walnut, birch or pine.
Hardware: Brass bales and escutcheons in a dull smoky finish.

Top _____ 1 pc. ⅞ x 21⅛ x 44
Ends _____ 2 pc. ⅞ x 20 x 34
End feet _____ 2 pc. ⅞ x 4 x 20⅞
Front feet _____ 1 pc. ⅞ x 4 x 43½
Upper drawer front ___ 1 pc. ⅞ x 5 x 40
Second drawer front __ 1 pc. ⅞ x 6 x 40
Third drawer front ___ 1 pc. ⅞ x 7½ x 40
Lower drawer front ___ 1 pc. ⅞ x 10½ x 40
Front rails in all frames, between drawers ___ 5 pc. 1 x 2½ x 40½
Back rails in all frames between drawers ___ 5 pc. 1 x 1½ x 40½
All crosspieces in all frames between drawers ___ 15 pc. 1 x 2 x 17¾
Drawer bottoms ___ 4 pc. ½ x 18½ x 39½
Upper drawer sides ___ 2 pc. ½ x 5 x 18½
Second drawer sides ___ 2 pc. ½ x 6 x 18½
Third drawer sides ___ 2 pc. ½ x 7½ x 18½
Lower drawer sides ___ 2 pc. ½ x 10½ x 18½
Upper drawer back ___ 1 pc. ½ x 3⅞ x 39½
Second drawer back ___ 1 pc. ½ x 4⅞ x 39½
Third drawer back ___ 1 pc. ½ x 6⅜ x 39½
Lower drawer back ___ 1 pc. ½ x 9⅜ x 39½
Guides for center runs, fastened to frames ___ 4 pc. ⅜ x 1 x 18½
Half-round molding ___ ½ inch about 28 feet
Back of chest ___ ¾ x 38 x 41
Strips "F" for drawer guides ___ 8 pc. ⁵⁄₁₆ x 1 x 18½
Strips for inside face of feet { 1 pc. 1 x 1½ x 39 / 2 pc. 1 x 1½ x 18
Molding on top edge of feet { 1 pc. 43½ long / 2 pc. 20⅞ long

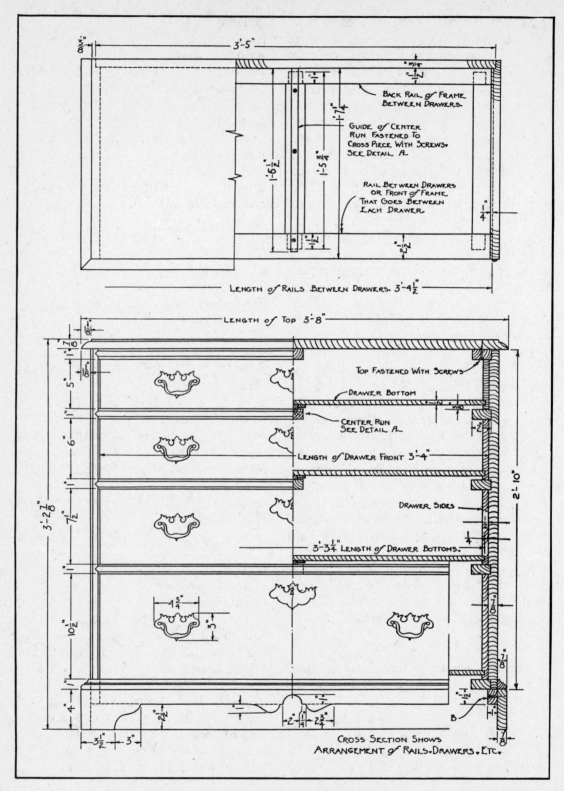

Plate 34. Front and Top Views of Chest of Drawers

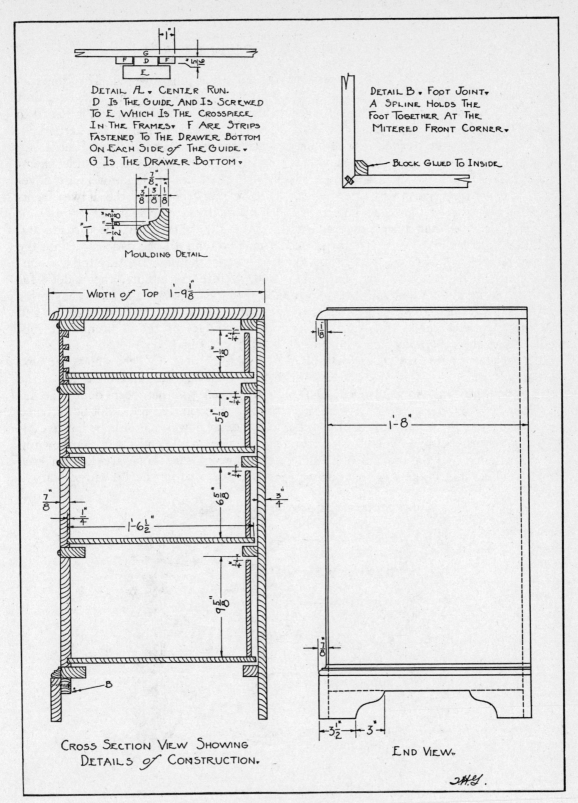

DETAIL A. CENTER RUN.
D IS THE GUIDE AND IS SCREWED
TO E WHICH IS THE CROSSPIECE
IN THE FRAMES. F ARE STRIPS
FASTENED TO THE DRAWER BOTTOM
ON EACH SIDE OF THE GUIDE.
G IS THE DRAWER BOTTOM.

DETAIL B. FOOT JOINT.
A SPLINE HOLDS THE
FOOT TOGETHER AT THE
MITERED FRONT CORNER.

BLOCK GLUED TO INSIDE

MOULDING DETAIL

WIDTH OF TOP 1-9⅛"

CROSS SECTION VIEW SHOWING
DETAILS OF CONSTRUCTION.

END VIEW.

Plate 35. End View Details of Chest of Drawers

SLANT-TOP SECRETARY

The finest kind of wood that possibly could be used to build the secretary is curly maple. It is more prized and more beautiful than bird's-eye maple, and if a desk like this one is made of it it will be more valuable than one made of mahogany. If curly maple is used, it should be finished with only a clear varnish or white shellac.

The lower part of the Slant-Top Secretary is little more than a chest of drawers, and the construction is essentially the same as that on the chest of drawers in this book. The end boards are glued up first, and dadoed on the inside to a depth of ¼ inch so that the frames between drawers may be fitted to them and held securely in place. The piece forming the front feet has a tongue or tenon cut on each end, by means of which it is fastened to the end boards with glue, as shown in detail D-D.

Each large drawer is guided by means of a center run as on the chest of drawers. This insures easy sliding. The upper drawer is shortened to make room on each side for the slides and keepers G that support the lid when it is lowered. The construction at E shows how the board, against which the upper drawer closes, is joined to the ends. Also notice how the keepers G, which are screwed to the end boards, are made. They are as long as the slides themselves. The sides of the drawers are dovetailed to the fronts, and the drawer fronts have a molded lip around each edge.

After the frames have been made and assembled, and all the dadoes cut into the end boards, the desk is ready to be assembled. Before assembling, the dadoes for the table board as well as the grooves for the tenons at D-D and E must be cut and the back edges of the ends must be rabbeted for the back.

When the desk has been glued, the next step is to cut dovetails and fit the top of the desk. When this has been done, the lid should be made. It should not be fastened to the desk, however, until the inside cabinet has been made and fitted. As shown in the drawing, small lips are left on each end board to cover the lid at the bottom.

Fig. 16. Slant-Top Secretary

The cabinet requires painstaking care in its construction. First, the three horizontal boards should be cut and dadoed for the vertical pieces forming the walls of the pigeonholes, and then all other partitions should be cut and fitted. These may be glued together before they are fitted to the desk. Very careful work must be done at this stage because faulty construction is very noticeable on the cabinet. The building of it is a test of real skill. Details of the construction of the small drawers are given so that very little trouble should be experienced in making them. Piece A forming the arches over the lower pigeonholes must be set in so its face side is flush with the front edges of the pigeonholes.

The desk is now completed, save for fitting the lid and hardware.

BILL OF MATERIAL

Ends	2 pc.	1	x 19	x 43
Top	1 pc.	1	x 11½	x 38
Lid	1 pc.	⅞	x 13½	x 36½
Cleats for lid	2 pc.	⅞	x 2	x 13½
Upper drawer front	1 pc.	⅞	x 4	x 32½
Second drawer front	1 pc.	⅞	x 5	x 36½
Third drawer front	1 pc.	⅞	x 5½	x 36½
Lower drawer front	1 pc.	⅞	x 6½	x 36½
Board against which upper drawer closes	1 pc.	1	x 5½	x 37½
Board for front feet	1 pc.	1	x 6½	x 37½
Table board on which inside cabinet rests	1 pc.	1	x 18¼	x 36½
Slides to support lid	2 pc.	¾	x 2	x 18¼
Block to hold slide (see G)	2 pc.	1¼	x 3½	x 17¼
Sides for upper drawer	2 pc.	½	x 3½	x 18¼
Sides for second drawer	2 pc.	½	x 4½	x 18¼
Sides for third drawer	2 pc.	½	x 5	x 18¼
Sides for lower drawer	2 pc.	½	x 6	x 18¼
Bottom for top drawer	1 pc.	½	x 17⅜	x 31½
Bottom for three lower drawers	3 pc.	½	x 17⅜	x 35½
Upper drawer back	1 pc.	½	x 2½	x 31½
Second drawer back	1 pc.	½	x 3½	x 35½
Third drawer back	1 pc.	½	x 4	x 35½
Lower drawer back	1 pc.	½	x 5	x 35½
Front rails for all frames	4 pc.	1	x 2	x 36½
Back rails for all frames	4 pc.	1	x 2	x 36½
End crosspieces for upper and lower frames	4 pc.	1	x 3¼	x 16¼
End crosspieces for middle frames	4 pc.	1	x 2½	x 17¼
Center crosspieces for upper and lower frames	2 pc.	1	x 2	x 16¼
Center crosspieces for middle frames	2 pc.	1	x 2	x 17¼
Long horizontal boards in cabinet	3 pc.	⅜	x 9	x 35½
Vertical end pieces on cabinet	2 pc.	⅜	x 9	x 11½
Vertical partitions in upper pigeonholes*	7 pc.	¼	x 9	x 4⅞
All lower vertical partitions	5 pc.	¼	x 9	x 6
Piece (A)	1 pc.	⅜	x 1⅞	x 15¼
Drawer fronts in cabinet	4 pc.	⅝	x 2¾	x 10
Drawer sides	8 pc.	⅜	x 2¾	x 8¾
Drawer bottoms	4 pc.	¼	x 8⅝	x 9⅝
Drawer backs	4 pc.	¼	x 2¼	x 9⅝
Back		¾	x 37	x 42

*Grain runs vertically.

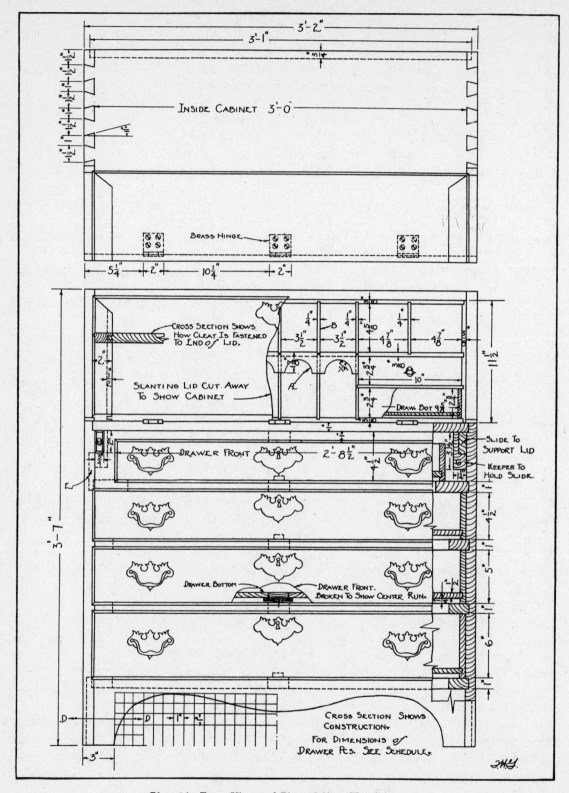

Plate 36. Front View and Plan of Slant-Top Secretary

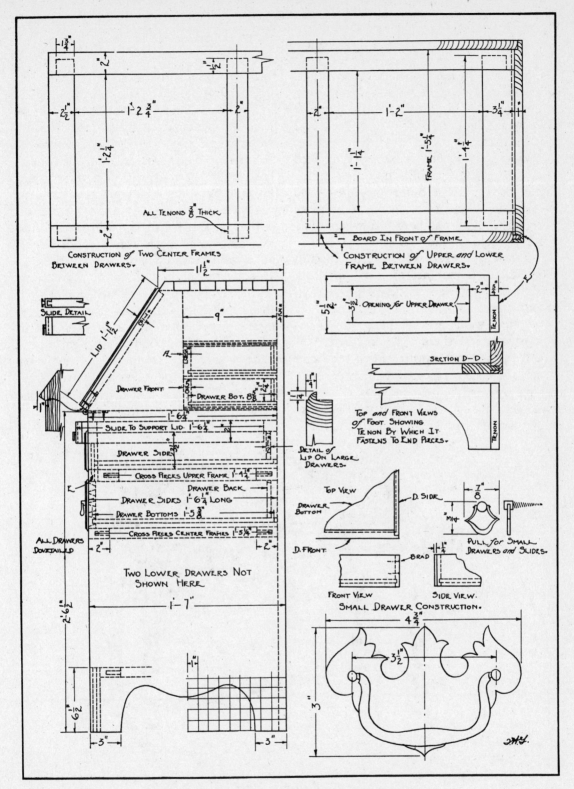

Plate 37. End View and Details of Slant-Top Secretary

EARLY AMERICAN DESK

The earliest home-manufactured desks in America were merely flat-topped boxes, sometimes with a hinged lid. Later, these lids were slanted so that the back was higher than the front, making it handier to write upon. These boxes were placed upon a small table and could be carried from place to place. Sometimes they were carried in front of the open fireplace where the light was best and where they could be held on the lap.

Later still, these boxes were fastened to small tables, sometimes merely nailed on, and finally they were made with legs as an integral part.

As time went on and the colonists became wealthier, there arose a greater demand for better furniture. Then the early square legs gave place to turned legs, the cabinet became more ornate, and beauty was sought as well as utility. Thus the metamorphosis progressed, until the finest form of desk, or "secretary" as it was called, resulted.

The desk here shown comes in the period somewhere between the lowliest wooden box and the stately secretary, so that it might be termed a transition piece. The design, of course, is original, but was inspired by some early pieces which the writer has measured.

This desk possesses a quality that often is lacking in modern examples, in that it has a well-braced frame and sturdy construction throughout. It is far more beautiful than the spinet desk, which at best is little more than a mongrel production, being neither a desk nor a musical instrument. This desk is light in weight and is made sturdy with long tenons and deep mortises, firmly joined with glue and stout oak pins. The top is joined to the ends with dovetail construction, which makes it as secure as though it had grown there.

Fig. 17. Early American Desk

The joints between the legs and the end pieces are hardly perceptible, because they are joined in such a manner that they appear as one flat board across the entire width of the desk on the outside. This is accomplished with a tongue-and-groove joint. After the end pieces have been formed, the whole end of the desk, including short stretcher, legs, and board, is glued together and pinned wherever necessary. Before this can be done, however, a dado must be cut across each end piece on the inside to admit the table board. This should be carefully fitted so that a crack will not show after the desk has been joined together. The table board has nothing to do with holding the desk together. This function is performed by the dovetailed board at the top, the aprons under the drawer in front and under the panel in the back, and by the long, turned stretcher below. The ends fitting into the dadoes help to make the frame still more rigid.

When the frame has been assembled, drawer runs can be added and the drawer and slides made and fitted. Here attention is called to the fact that, while the drawer front and slides are molded on all four edges, they have a lip on the vertical edges only. This lip is not present either on the top edge or the bottom edge of these members, as shown at K. The reason for this is very apparent. In every antique desk of this type that the writer has ever seen, this precaution was not taken. Instead, the lip was added all around the drawer and slides. The slides were so made that they could be drawn out far enough so that the lid would not rest upon the lip. However, probably through carelessness, the lip usually was broken off either from dropping the lid on it or through some other mishap. Therefore, in designing this piece, the danger has been avoided as shown. (See also cross sections of drawer front.)

The molding used on the large drawer and slides, as well as on the lower edge of the crosspiece under the drawer, is a combination of the quarter round and fillet. As shown at D, the drawer runs are supported by small blocks fastened with glue and screws to the frame on the inside.

In constructing the lid, attention should be called to several things. The 3-inch cleats on either end insure strength, prevent warping, and prevent end grain from showing at those places. When closed, the lid is held by a lip resting on the sides and top board. There should be plenty of clearance so that the lid will not bind when it is being opened or closed, as shown at M. The brass hinges should be large and strong and should be set into the wood so that they will come flush with the table top. If this is not done, they will mar the appearance, since they are placed in a very noticeable position.

The inside cabinet, consisting of pigeonholes, small drawers, etc., is made as a separate unit and, after being completed, can be fastened by means of a few small brads placed where they will not show; as for instance, beneath the small drawers. As shown in the detail, the small drawers have a narrow bead carved around the edges. The panel effect in the small door is produced by carving, shown in the contour at A-A. The door is held closed by means of a friction catch, shown at C.

The panel in the back of the desk is held in position, as shown at E. It may be made of good dry pine, but should have enough clearance at the joints to allow for swelling.

Correct hardware, in an antique or dull finish, is an important item in making this piece. Walnut or maple is the appropriate wood to use. A complete schedule of material is given in the following.

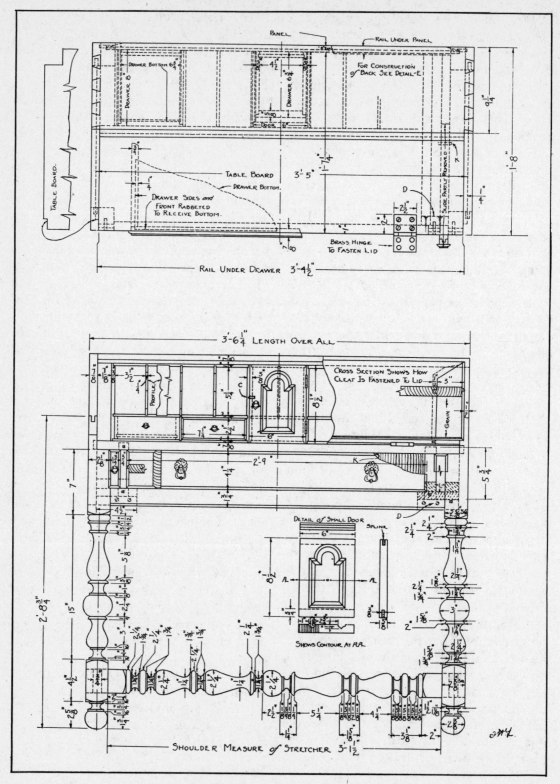

Plate 38. Plan and Front View of Early American Slant-Top Desk

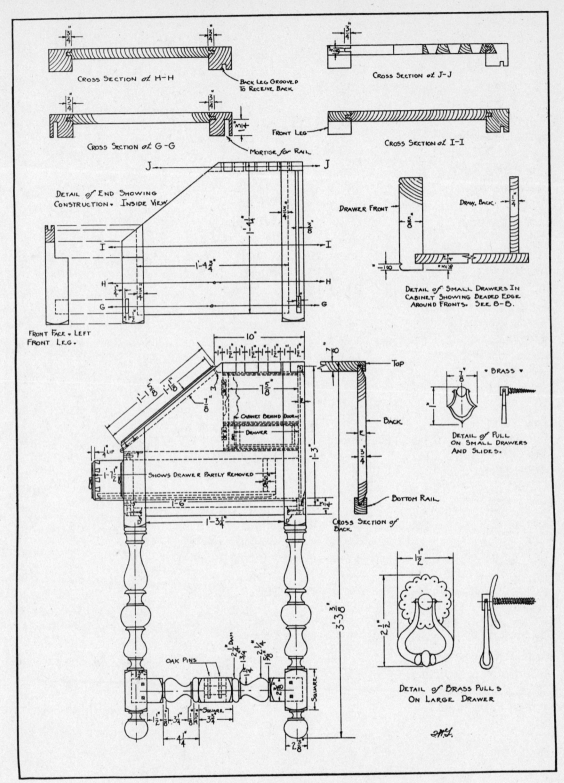

Plate 39. End View and Details of Early American Slant-Top Desk

BILL OF MATERIAL

Top _____ 1 pc. $\frac{7}{8}$ x 10   x 42$\frac{1}{4}$

Sides of desk* _____ 2 pc. $\frac{7}{8}$ x 16$\frac{3}{4}$ x 16$\frac{1}{4}$

Table board _____ 1 pc. $\frac{7}{8}$ x 19$\frac{1}{4}$ x 41

Apron under larg-
er drawer** _____ 1 pc. 1   x 1$\frac{3}{4}$ x 40$\frac{1}{2}$

Apron under panel
in back of desk __ 1 pc. 1   x 1$\frac{3}{4}$ x 40$\frac{1}{2}$

Stile between large
drawer and slides 2 pc. 1   x 1$\frac{1}{4}$ x 5$\frac{3}{4}$

Hinged lid _____ 1 pc. $\frac{7}{8}$ x 13$\frac{5}{8}$ x 41$\frac{1}{4}$

Cleats on end of
lid _____ 2 pc. $\frac{7}{8}$ x 3$\frac{1}{2}$ x 13$\frac{5}{8}$

Back legs*** _____ 2 pc. 3   x 3   x 39$\frac{3}{8}$

Front legs _____ 2 pc. 3   x 3   x 32$\frac{3}{4}$

Short stretchers ____ 2 pc. 2$\frac{3}{8}$ x 2$\frac{3}{8}$ x 18$\frac{3}{4}$

Long stretcher ____ 1 pc. 2$\frac{3}{8}$ x 2$\frac{3}{8}$ x 40$\frac{1}{2}$

Large drawer
front _____ 1 pc. $\frac{7}{8}$ x 4$\frac{1}{4}$ x 33

Large drawer
sides _____ 2 pc. $\frac{3}{4}$ x 4$\frac{1}{4}$ x 19

Large drawer
back _____ 1 pc. $\frac{5}{8}$ x 3$\frac{1}{2}$ x 32

Large drawer
bottom _____ 1 pc. $\frac{5}{8}$ x 19   x 32

Slides _____ 2 pc. $\frac{7}{8}$ x 4$\frac{1}{4}$ x 12$\frac{3}{4}$

Molded faces for
slides _____ 2 pc. 1   x 1$\frac{3}{4}$ x 4$\frac{1}{4}$

Small door in cabi-
net _____ 1 pc. $\frac{5}{8}$ x 6   x 8$\frac{1}{2}$

Runs for large
drawer and slides 2 pc. $\frac{7}{8}$ x 4$\frac{1}{2}$ x 18

Guides between
large drawer and
slides _____ 2 pc. $\frac{7}{8}$ x 1$\frac{1}{4}$ x 18

Guides on outside
of slides _____ 2 pc. $\frac{7}{8}$ x 1$\frac{1}{2}$ x 18

End partitions in
inside cabinet ____ 2 pc. $\frac{3}{8}$ x 8$\frac{1}{4}$ x 8$\frac{1}{2}$

Longest horizontal
pieces over and
under small
drawer and pi-
geonholes _____ 6 pc. $\frac{1}{4}$ x 8$\frac{1}{4}$ x 15

Partitions dividing
small drawers
from door _____ 2 pc. $\frac{5}{8}$ x 8$\frac{1}{4}$ x 8$\frac{1}{2}$

Vertical partitions
between pigeon-
holes _____ 7 pc. $\frac{1}{4}$ x 8$\frac{1}{4}$ x 5$\frac{3}{8}$

Vertical partitions
between small
drawers _____ 2 pc. $\frac{1}{2}$ x 8$\frac{1}{4}$ x 2$\frac{5}{8}$

Horizontal parti-
tions back of
small door _____ 3 pc. $\frac{1}{4}$ x 6$\frac{3}{4}$ x 5$\frac{5}{8}$

Small drawer
fronts _____ 4 pc. $\frac{5}{8}$ x 2$\frac{1}{2}$ x 7$\frac{1}{4}$

Small drawer
front behind
door _____ 1 pc. $\frac{5}{8}$ x 2$\frac{1}{2}$ x 5$\frac{1}{4}$

Small drawer
sides _____ 8 pc. $\frac{3}{8}$ x 2$\frac{1}{2}$ x 7$\frac{7}{8}$

Small drawer sides
back of door ____ 2 pc. $\frac{3}{8}$ x 2$\frac{1}{2}$ x 6$\frac{5}{8}$

Small drawer
backs _____ 4 pc. $\frac{1}{4}$ x 2   x 6$\frac{3}{4}$

Back of small
drawer behind
door _____ 1 pc. $\frac{1}{4}$ x 2   x 4$\frac{5}{8}$

Small drawer bot-
toms _____ 4 pc. $\frac{1}{4}$ x 6$\frac{3}{4}$ x 7$\frac{1}{2}$

Bottom for small
drawer behind
door _____ 1 pc. $\frac{1}{4}$ x 4$\frac{5}{8}$ x 6$\frac{1}{4}$

Panel in back of
desk _____ 1 pc. $\frac{3}{4}$ x 15   x 38$\frac{1}{2}$

---

*This includes the tongue that fits into the
    leg.

**This includes the length of the tenons.

***Largest diam. given for thickness.

SMALL CHEST ON FRAME

The small chest on frame is in reality a modified highboy, and is an interesting piece of furniture in several respects. It is very attractive because it is not very tall, differing in this respect from many pieces of its kind. It also is designed along very simple lines, making it suitable for the average small home. It may be used in the living room, hallway, or bedroom.

The construction of the upper part does not differ very much from that of the chest of drawers in the preceding problem. As described in that problem, these drawers are supported on frames which are put together before the chest is assembled, and are guided on center runs. The details of the center runs on this piece will be made clear by an examination of the drawing.

When making the chest on frame, the table or lower part should be made and assembled first. No explanation as to the procedure is necessary if the drawing is studied. It may be well to call attention to the fact that the lower edges of the aprons are molded.

The oval-type drawer pulls are to be used on this piece. The oak-leaf-and-acorn pattern is shown in the drawing.

BILL OF MATERIAL

Item	Qty	Dimensions
Top	1 pc.	$7/8$ x $21\frac{1}{4}$ x 37
End boards of chest	2 pc.	$7/8$ x 19 x $32\frac{1}{8}$
Lower drawer front	1 pc.	$7/8$ x $7\frac{1}{2}$ x $30\frac{3}{4}$
Second drawer front	1 pc.	$7/8$ x 7 x $30\frac{3}{4}$
Third drawer front	1 pc.	$7/8$ x 6 x $30\frac{3}{4}$
Upper drawer front	1 pc.	$7/8$ x 5 x $30\frac{3}{4}$
Front and back apron below drawer	2 pc.	$7/8$ x $4\frac{1}{2}$ x $33\frac{1}{2}$
End aprons	2 pc.	$7/8$ x $4\frac{1}{2}$ x $18\frac{1}{2}$
Legs	4 pc.	$2\frac{3}{4}$ x $2\frac{3}{4}$ x 28
Long turned stretcher	1 pc.	$2\frac{3}{4}$ x $2\frac{3}{4}$ x $33\frac{1}{2}$
Short turned end stretchers	2 pc.	$2\frac{3}{4}$ x $2\frac{3}{4}$ x $18\frac{1}{2}$
Long front rails on frames between drawers	5 pc.	1 x $2\frac{1}{2}$ x $31\frac{1}{4}$
Rear rails on frames between drawers	5 pc.	1 x 2 x $31\frac{1}{4}$
End and center rails on frames between drawers	15 pc.	1 x 2 x $17\frac{1}{4}$
Center runs	5 pc.	$\frac{5}{16}$ x 1 x $17\frac{3}{8}$
Drawer bottoms	4 pc.	$3/8$ x $17\frac{1}{2}$ x $30\frac{1}{4}$

Fig. 18. Small Chest on Frame

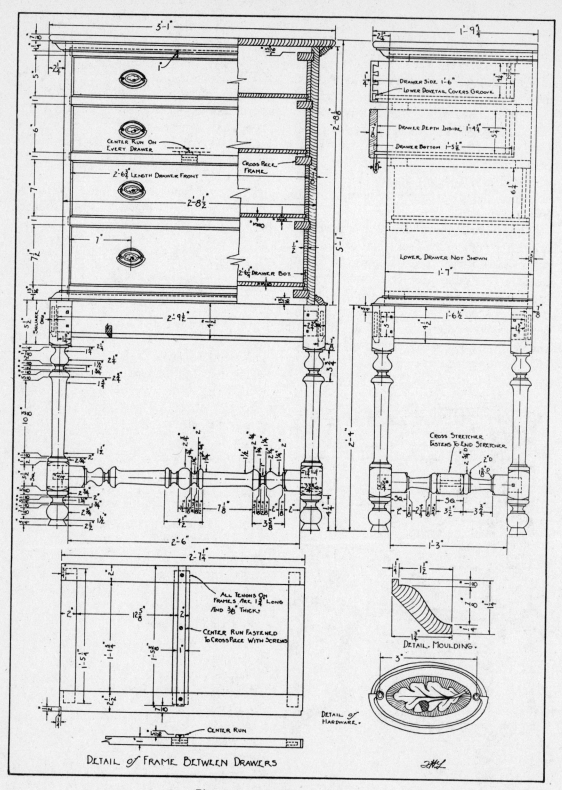

Plate 40. Small Chest on Frame

Lower drawer
sides _____2 pc. ½ x 7½ x 18

Second drawer
sides _____2 pc. ½ x 7   x 18

Third drawer
sides _____2 pc. ½ x 6   x 18

Top drawer sides _ 2 pc. ½ x 5   x 18

Lower drawer
back _____1 pc. ½ x 6¾ x 30¼

Second drawer
back _____1 pc. ½ x 6¼ x 30¼

Third drawer
back _____1 pc. ½ x 5¼ x 30¼

Upper drawer
back _____1 pc. ½ x 4¼ x 30¼

Molding, about 14 feet

Back _____   ¾ x 31⅝ x 32⅛

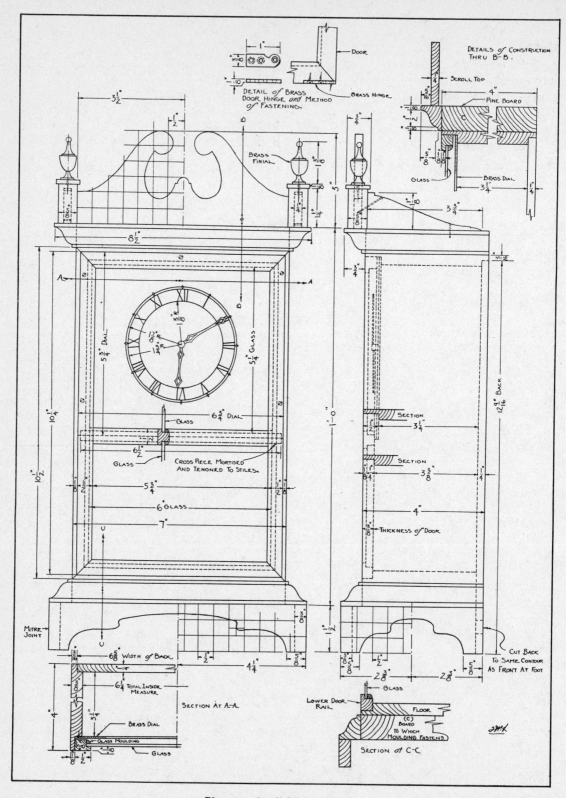

Plate 41. Small Mantel Clock

SMALL MANTEL CLOCK

The small mantel clock which should be made of mahogany, is not too difficult a project for the home craftsman or the high-school student.

When all the stock has been cut, the sides, top, and floor board should be dressed, and one edge of each rabbeted ¼ inch for the back to fit into. In the drawing, the front edge of the top is rabbeted ½ inch deep while the bottom is rabbeted to a depth of only ⅜ inch, and the sides are rabbeted ½ inch from the top down as far as the dial extends. From there to the floor the sides are rabbeted only ⅜ inch deep, permitting the door to close only against the lower part. The upper part is rabbeted deeper to make a place for the dial.

The dial should be enameled white or ivory. If possible, it should be ordered from a clock company with the works of the clock. In ordering the works the inside dimensions of the case should be given.

When the sides, top, and bottom have been rabbeted, they must be mitered at each end and glued and bradded together. They should be bradded only from the top and bottom, because these pieces are covered with the boards, to which the molding is fastened.

Now the main case should be made. First, the boards C should be fastened with screws to the case and then the molding. When this has been done, the pattern for the feet and the scrolled top should be made. The feet should be miter-joined at the front corners, and dadoed at the rear end to receive the back.

The pedestals should be fastened, and then the scrolled top may be fastened between the pedestals with brackets or strips from behind.

The door is not difficult to make if care is exercised. Constructing it involves practically the same procedure as that followed when making a picture frame. The door should be hinged by means of small, flat brass hinges, as shown in detail E. When completed, the clock should be finished in a red-mahogany color.

BILL OF MATERIAL

Scrolled top	1 pc.	¼ x 3 x 7
Pedestals u n d e r finials	2 pc.	⅝ x ⅝ x 1¼
Caps for pedestals	2 pc.	⅛ x ¾ x ¾
Sides of clock	2 pc.	⅜ x 4 x 10½
Stiles of door	2 pc.	⅜ x ½ x 10¼
Rails of door	3 pc.	⅜ x ½ x 6¾
Top and floor of clock	2 pc.	⅜ x 4 x 7
Front of feet	1 pc.	⅜ x 1½ x 8½
Side feet	2 pc.	⅜ x 1½ x 4¾
Boards above top and under floor*	2 pc.	¾ x 4 x 7
Molding		about 3 feet
Side pieces in top	2 pc.	¼ x 1⅛ x 3¾
Back (pine)		¼ x 6⅝ x 12 9/16
M i d d l e cross-piece		⅜ x ½ x 6½

*These boards may be made of any soft wood.

A COLONIAL MANTEL CLOCK

The Colonial Mantel Clock illustrated here and in the frontispiece is a fine example of the good taste and the creative ability of Early American cabinetmakers. In working this out, the writer has very closely followed a design which he saw in New England and has made very few changes. Some improvements have been made in the shape of the bonnet scrolls, the urn finials, and the quarter columns. These follow correct design, which calls for finials shaped like urns, with graceful stems, while the quarter columns should follow architectural forms. The Roman-Tuscan order has been very closely followed in the design.

The fine molding, the perfect symmetry and balance, the shapely bracket foot, the fine, hand-painted dial, and the beautiful inlay, all help to make this truly a gem of the cabinetmakers' art.

It has indeed been a true pleasure to work this piece up into a comprehensive working drawing which it is hoped will be of benefit to craftsmen who want to make really fine pieces.

A movement for this clock case can be purchased from several manufacturers. The original case contained a weight clock. While this would be the more nearly correct, there is no reason why a spring clock would not do just as well, but in ordering a movement the size of the case must be given.

To make the construction perfectly clear to the maker, great pains have been taken to neglect no detail, and many cross-section views have been made. This has been found to be the clearest and most satisfactory way of showing construction.

The case is made of mahogany throughout, but walnut may be used as well, if so desired. In the lower door, the grain of the wood is formed into a very beautiful candle-flame effect. In order to obtain this result, a crotch-mahogany board, about 8 inches wide and 11 inches long, should be ripped through the middle, and then, after turning one piece over, should be glued up to give the desired effect. The joint is made stronger by running a spline from top to bottom.

When this has been done, the case should be rabbeted for the inlay and veneer, which can be purchased ready for use. The veneer in this case is glued on with the grain perpendicular to the molding, which is afterward applied around the edge.

The glass door is outlined with a narrow band of inlay, and the feet also are trimmed with inlay which can be made of any light-colored, straight-grained hard wood. The door molding also has a bead around the inside edge. In the arch of the door this bead will have to be carved by hand.

The simplest way to make the quarter columns is to glue four $7/8$-inch square strips together, with pieces of fairly heavy drawing paper between them. After the full column has been turned, it may be easily split into quarter sections, provided the exact center has been maintained when it was centered on the lathe. This overcomes the difficulty that would be met in cutting too wide a kerf when ripping a small column with a band saw.

In the sections at A-A and B-B the construction of the lower case of the clock is clearly illustrated. The stock used in the sides is $1/2$ inch thick. The front is a frame made of stock $5/8$ inch thick, and is mortised and tenoned together. It is then fastened to the sides by means of pieces H and I which should be made of well-dried pine or poplar. These pieces are covered and hidden by the quarter column.

The section at C-C shows how the upper cabinet is constructed. It shows the method of fastening the hand-painted dial which is made of brass, about 16 gauge or heavier. The dial is screwed to the sides which have been rabbeted deeply to receive it and the door. The back of the clock is made of pine boards 3/8 inch thick.

In the section at E-E the construction of the bonnet top is shown. Instead of using wood to cover the mechanism, it has been found more satisfactory to use wall board, as shown at J. This is soaked in water for a short time so that it will bend easily, and then is nailed to the back and to K. K is made of soft pine and serves as a backing for the molding L. It is curved to the same shape as this molding, but its ends are formed into forks which hook over and fasten to the sides, as shown in detail K. A detail of the molding is shown, and all the molding except that immediately above the feet is made in this fashion, although sometimes only a section of it is used as in the molding around the lower door and the moldings M and N in the section at F-F. In the cross section at G-G, O is shown, which is made of pine and, when fastened to the lower case, forms a support for the upper case to rest upon.

The hinges and hardware are of brass finished in a special old color. These should never be a bright brass which looks common and out of place on a clock of this kind. Following is a complete list of the stock required for this clock.

BILL OF MATERIAL

Lower Case

Sides of lower case, mahogany ... 2 pc. $\frac{1}{2}$ x $4\frac{1}{2}$ x 14
Lower rail of front frame, mahogany ... 1 pc. $\frac{5}{8}$ x $1\frac{3}{4}$ x $9\frac{1}{4}$
Top rail of front frame, mahogany ... 1 pc. $\frac{5}{8}$ x $1\frac{5}{8}$ x $9\frac{1}{4}$
Side rails of front frame, mahogany ... 2 pc. $\frac{5}{8}$ x $\frac{7}{8}$ x 14

Lower Door

Crotch mahogany 1 pc. $\frac{1}{2}$ x $7\frac{7}{8}$ x $10\frac{5}{8}$

Feet

Front, mahogany 1 pc. $\frac{1}{2}$ x $1\frac{1}{2}$ x $11\frac{3}{4}$
Sides, mahogany ... 2 pc. $\frac{1}{2}$ x $1\frac{1}{2}$ x $5\frac{1}{2}$
Back, pine cut same shape as front feet ... 1 pc. $\frac{1}{2}$ x $1\frac{1}{2}$ x $11\frac{3}{4}$

Floor

Soft pine ... 1 pc. $\frac{1}{2}$ x $4\frac{1}{4}$ x $10\frac{3}{4}$

Column

To be glued together and turned, mahogany ... 4 pc. $\frac{7}{8}$ x $\frac{7}{8}$ x $9\frac{5}{8}$
Pedestals under column P, mahogany ... 2 pc. $\frac{3}{4}$ x $\frac{3}{4}$ x $2\frac{7}{8}$
Blocks over column Q, mahogany ... 2 pc. $\frac{3}{4}$ x $\frac{3}{4}$ x $1\frac{1}{4}$
Thin blocks over and under columns, mahogany 4 pc. $\frac{1}{8}$ x $\frac{7}{8}$ x $\frac{7}{8}$
Molding around door ... about $3\frac{1}{2}$ feet
Molding S ... about 2 feet
H in cross section at B-B pine ... 2 pc. $\frac{1}{2}$ x $\frac{3}{4}$ x $13\frac{1}{2}$
I in cross section at B-B pine ... 2 pc. $\frac{1}{4}$ x $\frac{5}{8}$ x $13\frac{1}{2}$

Upper Case

Sides for top case, mahogany ... 2 pc. $\frac{5}{8}$ x $4\frac{1}{2}$ x 12

Door

Lower rail, mahogany ... 1 pc. $\frac{1}{2}$ x 1 x $8\frac{5}{8}$
Long vertical pieces, mahogany 2 pc. $\frac{1}{2}$ x 1 x $9\frac{3}{4}$

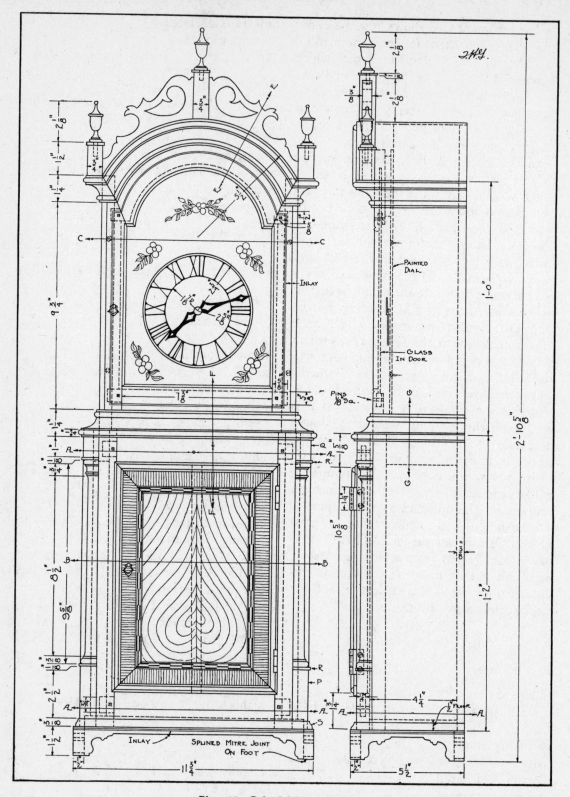

Plate 42. Colonial Mantel Clock

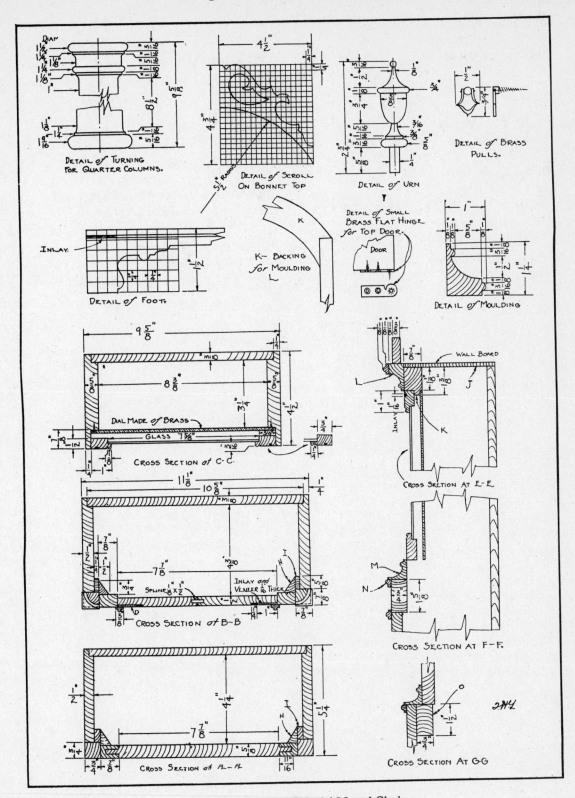

Plate 43. Details of Colonial Mantel Clock

Arch of door, must
be cut out of piece
this size, mahog-
any _____1 pc. ½ x 4   x 8⅝

Finials

Small flat blocks
under finials, ma-
hogany _____3 pc. ⅛ x ⅞ x ⅞
Blocks under out-
side finials, ma-
hogany _____2 pc. ¾ x ¾ x 1½
Block under center
finial, mahogany 1 pc. ¾ x ¾ x 2⅛
F i n i a l s, mahog-
any _____3 pc. ¾ (greatest diam.) x 2¾

Scrolls

Scrolls, mahogany 2 pc. ⅜ x 4½ x 4¾
Piece marked K in
cross section at E-
E, pine _____1 pc. ⅞ x 4   x 10
Arched   molding
under s c r o l l s
(stock before cut-
ting) _____1 pc. 1   x 4   x 10
Approximate length of molding needed for
sides of top and between upper and
lower cabinet _____3½ feet
Approximate size
of back of clock,
pine _____1 pc. ⅜ x 11   x 29

CHINA CABINET

The China Cabinet is a problem that will test the skill of any advanced home craftsman or student in cabinetmaking. The greatest difficulty that will be encountered in its construction is in making the door. The cabinet has been designed so that every piece used in its construction may be made by the home craftsman on simple machinery or by the student with the machines usually found in the average school shop. For this reason, standard sash molding should not be used in making the door, because it would require special machinery.

The cabinet itself is simple. The pieces making up the case are first cut to size and dressed. These pieces include the ceiling, the floor, the two ends, the two vertical pieces back of the pilasters, the rails above and below the door, and the back. The end pieces as well as the top and bottom are

Fig. 12. China Cabinet

rabbeted along the back edge to receive the back. After this has been done, the cabinet is nailed together with finishing nails. The rails above and below the door are mortised and tenoned to the vertical pieces back of the pilasters.

The next step consists of making a pattern for the scrolled pediment, which is then made and nailed in place. The rosettes are turned next and glued to the pediment. The strips D which are ⅜ inch thick and ½ inch wide, are cut on the band saw to conform to the shape of the pediment, and then are glued to the top edge of the pediment. They are mitered where they meet the return strip fastened on each end. The finial is turned on a lathe and fastened by boring a ⅜-inch hole in the pediment and gluing. The dentils G are fastened last of all with brads.

Next, the pilasters are made. These are merely flat boards ¾ inch thick, each one having four flutes. They have a base made of a block 1¼ inches thick and a cap made of a board ⅜ inch thick. The molding used on the pilasters may be bought, but since there is not much of it, it is advisable to make it, using a combination molding plane. The pilasters are nailed to the cabinet.

The two shelves are adjustable to different levels. This adjustment is made possible by fastening vertical strips B in each of the four corners, having notches cut at different levels. These notches support a small stick C upon which the shelves rest.

The final step consists of making the door. The molding for this also may be cut by hand with a combination plane. A study of the door detail in the drawing will make the construction clear. The narrow molding should be made in one long piece and afterward sawed to the lengths need-

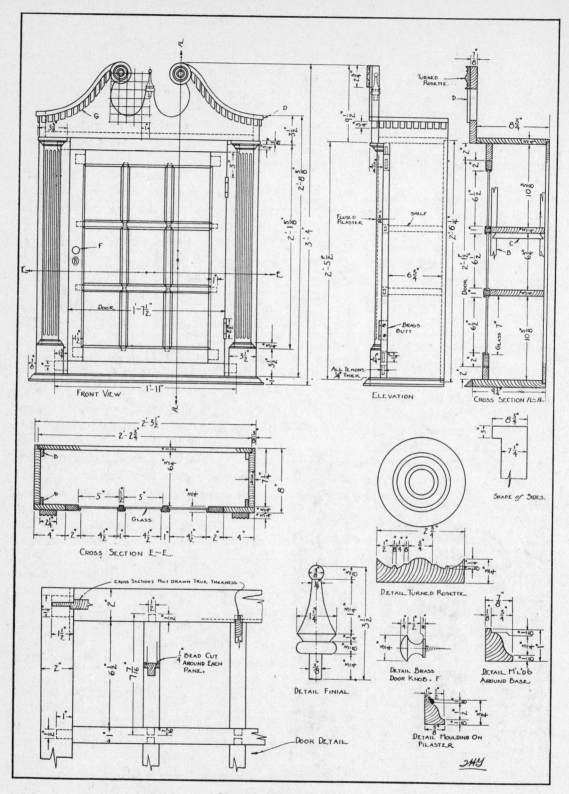

Plate 44. China Cabinet

ed. The construction of the door in the cabinet is essentially the same as that found on all French doors. The molding is different from the standard sash molding, and because of its greater width is not so difficult to join together. It will be found best to cut the beading on the door with a wood carver's V tool and a skew chisel, after it has been assembled.

When the cabinet has been finished, it should be painted white or ivory. All nail holes should be puttied after the priming coat, which consists of a light application of inside white paint. This coat should be followed with two coats of paint and one or two coats of enamel. Forty-eight hours should be allowed for each coat to dry, and each coat should be carefully sanded with 2/0 sandpaper before the next is applied.

BILL OF MATERIAL

Scrolled top ....1 pc. $\frac{7}{8}$ x $9\frac{1}{2}$ x $27\frac{1}{2}$
Stiles to which pilasters fasten ......2 pc. $\frac{3}{4}$ x 4 x $29\frac{1}{2}$
Cross rails under and over door ....2 pc. $\frac{3}{4}$ x 2 x 23
Fluted pilasters ..2 pc. $\frac{3}{4}$ x $2\frac{1}{4}$ x $25\frac{5}{8}$
Pedestals under pilasters ....2 pc. $1\frac{1}{4}$ x $3\frac{1}{2}$ x $3\frac{1}{2}$
Cap above pilasters ....2 pc. $\frac{3}{8}$ x $1\frac{3}{4}$ x $3\frac{3}{4}$
Sides of cabinet....2 pc. $\frac{3}{4}$ x $7\frac{1}{4}$ x $32\frac{5}{8}$
Floor of cabinet....1 pc. 1 x $9\frac{1}{4}$ x $27\frac{1}{2}$
Ceiling of cabinet..1 pc. $\frac{3}{4}$ x $8\frac{3}{4}$ x 26
Shelves ....2 pc. $\frac{3}{4}$ x $6\frac{3}{4}$ x 26
Rosettes ....2 pc. $\frac{3}{4}$ x $2\frac{3}{4}$ diam.
Back of cabinet.... $\frac{1}{2}$ x $26\frac{3}{4}$ x $30\frac{1}{4}$
Outside door stiles 2 pc. $\frac{3}{4}$ x 2 x $25\frac{1}{2}$
Upper and lower door rails ....2 pc. $\frac{3}{4}$ x 2 x $18\frac{1}{2}$
Narrow door rails..2 pc. $\frac{3}{4}$ x 1 x $17\frac{1}{2}$
Small vertical piece in door ......6 pc. $\frac{3}{4}$ x 1 x $7\frac{7}{16}$
Dentils..............$\frac{1}{8}$ thick x $\frac{5}{8}$ wide. Length varies. Spaced $\frac{1}{4}$ apart.
Moldings, curved strips above dentils, etc.
Finial ....1 pc. $1\frac{1}{4}$ diam. x $3\frac{1}{2}$

PART III

FURNITURE FINISHING

FURNITURE FINISHING

WOOD finishing includes all operations which in any way change the surface appearance of wood or supply a coating that preserves it. As applied to furniture the term commonly includes such typical operations as preparing the surface by scraping and sanding, coloring with a dye or stain, filling the pores to seal them and provide a level surface, covering with a transparent coating of shellac, varnish, or lacquer, rubbing and polishing with a mild abrasive like rottenstone or pumice, and finally cleaning with preservative oil. An entirely different type of wood finishing consists in applying several coats of opaque materials like paint, enamel, or colored lacquer which entirely cover the wood and act as a protective coating.

Finishing is decidedly an art. So important is a working knowledge of the materials and operations employed, that a brief treatment like a single chapter in this book is entirely inadequate to familiarize the beginner with even the essentials of the art. It is felt, however, that in order to make this book more specifically helpful to the user, such a chapter must be included. It is suggested that the reader familiarize himself with at least one good book on the subject.

Very few cabinetmakers know how to finish their pieces. In modern manufacturing plants, it is entirely impractical for the cabinetmaker to do the finishing on the furniture he builds. This must be done in a separate department, by experienced finishers. The division of labor necessitated by the competitive situation in industry usually results in one man doing the staining and filling, another the varnishing, still another the rubbing down. Every student, apprentice, and home craftsman who builds a piece of furniture will be a better cabinetmaker if he can complete his project from beginning to end. For this reason every student and apprentice should know the rudiments of the art at least.

There are those who think that furniture designed in the early American or colonial style, like that suggested in this book, must be made to look old or "antiquated," in order to be correct. Nothing could be farther from the truth. Faking new furniture to pass it off as antique is wrong. Finishing a new piece of furniture in such a way that it appears worn and faded in spots, and "arting" it up in any way whatsoever in order that it may be sold as a faithful copy of an original, is almost as bad as faking, and can only be classed as misguided endeavor. Thus, the wearing down of sharp corners and edges with a file, treating wood with acids to make it seem of great age, artificially wearing down the feet of chairs—all these and many other subterfuges are nothing less than misapplied effort. The resulting wrecks can hardly be called sincere copies. Exact copies should reproduce all features as they originally were, and should not be defaced as the original one has become after long and hard service.

In most school and home shops, it is not practical to mix stains and finishing materials from complicated formulas. Fortunately, good prepared finishes may be bought at paint or hardware stores, which, if properly used, will provide the desired effect.

The first and one of the most important steps in finishing a piece of furniture is to prepare the surface. This is accomplished by scraping and sandpapering. Too much stress cannot be laid on the careful performance of this part of the work. Rough spots and marks, not previously noticed, will show plainly when stain has been applied. At least two grades of sandpaper should be used and the wood thoroughly sanded, working the sandpaper back and forth in the direction of the grain. The final sanding should be done with 2/0 sandpaper or even a finer grade. Methods of preparing old work for refinishing will be discussed later. When all marks have been removed and the surface is perfectly smooth, the work is ready for the next operation. What it will be depends upon two things: first, upon the kind of wood to be treated, and second, upon the kind of finish to be used.

Three kinds of stains on the market are good to use on new work. Besides these, there are so-called varnish stains, which usually are cheap varnish to which coloring matter has been added. They should never be used on high-grade furniture which deserves a good finish, because satisfactory work cannot be done with them. The three kinds of stain recommended by experienced finishers are water stains, penetrating (sometimes called spirit) stains, and oil stains. Water stains will be considered first.

Water stains are the cheapest of the three kinds and, if properly used, the best. They come in powder form, are soluble in water, and can be easily made up in any quantity according to the manufacturers' directions. They cannot very well be used to refinish old work, since wood that has been finished before will not absorb them. Specific directions for dissolving the dye in water are not given here because the methods vary with the different stains. Some must be dissolved in hot water, some in warm water, etc. When preparing them, the manufacturer's directions should be carefully followed for good results. Some of the advantages that recommend water stains are:

1. They give rich colors that will not fade.

2. They penetrate into the wood very deeply. This is the most important reason for their wide use.

3. They are very transparent, and do not hide but rather accentuate the beauty of the grain.

The most serious drawback in using any water stain is that it raises the grain of the wood to which it is applied. A surface which has been stained with a water stain must be sanded smooth again after the stain has dried. This sanding is usually done after a very thin wash coat of shellac has been applied. If a water stain is to be used, the wood must be prepared beforehand by sponging. To do this, a sponge must be moistened in cold water, and the entire piece of furniture gone over. After the wood has thoroughly dried, it must be sanded smooth with 2/0 sandpaper. Some finishers repeat this operation, but if carefully performed, the first application should suffice. The stain may then be applied and, after drying, sanded.

Penetrating stains, most of which are alcoholic stains, may be purchased ready-mixed. Like water stains, they penetrate well, at the same time raising the grain somewhat. The colors are very rich and transparent. The stains are so expensive, however, that they are not widely used, although some finishers prefer them and use them with good results.

Oil stains may be purchased ready-mixed, or in paste form. If in paste form, they must be mixed with turpentine or benzine to the required consistency. Usually one pound of paste will make a gallon of stain. The advantages of oil stains are:

1. A wide range of colors from which to choose is available.

2. They are obtainable at almost any hardware store.

3. They do not raise the grain.

4. They can be used to refinish old work.

5. They mix readily with fillers.

6. They can be made as light or as dark as desired, by mixing in different proportions with thinners.

7. They are not expensive.

8. They protect the wood, acting as primers and partly filling the grain of the wood.

Oil stains are only semitransparent and, therefore, hide the grain of the wood to some extent. They merely cover the surface, and do not penetrate the wood. Manufacturers of high-grade furniture do not like to use them, since there is an ever-present danger that a small dent or scratch will spoil an entire surface, necessitating the refinishing of the piece.

All stain may be applied with a good, long bristle brush, and wiped off with a clean cloth soon afterward. The surface to be stained should be placed in a convenient position before beginning operations, preferably on a low revolving platform. Cheap, unbleached muslin or sheeting is a good material to use in the finishing room for almost every purpose where cloth is required.

After the wood has been stained and allowed to dry about 24 hours, it is ready for filler. Only porous woods, such as oak, walnut, and mahogany, need fillers. Pine, gum, cedar, maple, and other close-grained woods do not need them. Fillers are of two kinds: liquid and paste. A paste filler gives the best results, but should be thinned with turpentine or benzine to the consistency of cream before using. Filler must be colored as nearly as possible like the stain that has been used. Its application then will not change the color of the piece of furniture. The filler should be applied liberally with a good, full, bristle brush, brushing across the grain, working it well into the pores of the wood. Sufficient time must be al-lowed for the filler to set, so that, in rubbing off with burlap or excelsior, the surplus will cut off clean with the surface and not be torn out of the pores of the wood. If, when rubbing the palm of the hand over the filled surface, it gathers and rolls up, it is ready to be rubbed off. When most of the surplus filler has been removed with burlap or excelsior, the remainder should be thoroughly rubbed off with muslin cloth. If an extra-fine job is desired, the filling operation should be repeated after 24 hours have elapsed. When the last coat of filler has dried for 24 hours, it should be sanded slightly with 2/0 sandpaper or an even finer grade. An oil filler can be used over any kind of stain.

The application of the filler is the last step in the staining process. It must be followed by the application of a protective film that will prevent heat, air, moisture, dirt, and wear from spoiling the surface. To accomplish this, two kinds of finish materials have been found satisfactory under present-day living and heating conditions. They are shellac and varnish. Their correct application will not only protect the surface, but also brings out the full beauty of the grain in the wood. Clear lacquer is also good when applied over a coat of shellac or on new wood. Since it is not possible to apply it with a brush and get good results, it is not recommended for use in the school or home workshop.

The first one to be considered is shellac finish. The beginner usually will obtain better results with shellac than with varnish because it is not so likely to fail. The advantages of shellac finish are:

1. Shellac is easy to apply.

2. It can be applied under a great variety of weather conditions.

3. A special dustproof room in which to do the work is not necessary. However, dust must be avoided as much as possible.

4. It dries very quickly.

5. It is easily obtainable and is low in cost.

To offset the advantages of a shellac finish, there are distinct disadvantages which must be considered before selecting this material:

1. Shellac does not long resist moisture and the direct action of sunlight. It cannot be used safely on articles which are placed outdoors where sun and rain attack them.

2. Heat mars it. Table tops which are likely to hold hot dishes, are easily ruined.

3. Alcohol and chemicals used in toilet waters, perfumes, etc., spoil shellac surfaces.

4. Shellac can be ruined by too much brushing which causes it to gum and heap up.

At least five applications are necessary to build up a good shellac finish. The first coat of shellac should be thinned to a consistency of about 2½ pounds of shellac gum to 1 gallon of alcohol. This is called a 2½-pound cut of shellac. For the succeeding coats, the cut may be from 3 to 4 pounds per gallon of alcohol. It should be remembered, however, that the best results are obtained by using many coats of thin shellac rather than a few coats of thick shellac. For the best results each coat must be allowed to dry 24 hours, and must be smoothed with 2/0 sandpaper or steel wool or both, before the succeeding coat is applied.

Varnish is the best protective finish for furniture, but it requires more care on the part of the operator than does shellac. It is not more difficult to apply than shellac, but more precautions must be taken in order that it may not go wrong. The advantages of varnish are:

1. Fewer coats are necessary to get a good finish than with shellac.

2. Varnish resists to a remarkable degree the action of heat, moisture, chemicals, grease, etc.

3. Varnish is very elastic and will not crack easily when a dent is made in the wood.

4. Varnish resists sun and air better than shellac.

One who uses varnish for the first time often becomes discouraged by failure, largely because he is not familiar with some of the precautions that must be exercised in its use. Following are listed several rules and precautions, also a few don'ts which, if kept in mind, should help the novice avoid most varnish troubles:

1. The grade of varnish recommended by the manufacturer for a particular type of job should be used. Varnish is manufactured in many grades, each intended for a different purpose.

2. Only as much varnish as is expected to be used should be poured from the can. What is left must, under no circumstances, be poured back since it may spoil the contents of the entire can. Rather than spoil the entire can, the leftover varnish should be destroyed or used for unimportant work.

3. The temperature of a room where varnishing is being done always should be at least 70 degrees F. For the best results the temperature should be a little higher, about 75 degrees F.

4. Since dust particles will adhere to a newly varnished surface as long as 5 hours after it has been applied, it is very important that the work be done in a dust-free room.

5. Each coat must be allowed to dry at least 48 hours before the succeeding coat is applied. Some long-oil varnishes require more time than that.

6. If a paint-and-varnish remover has been used on the surface of the wood and has not been sufficiently washed off with gasoline before the stain was applied, the varnish will blister.

7. Varnish which is poured into a container that is not clean, or that has been cleaned with paint-and-varnish remover, will probably not harden when applied.

8. The brush with which varnish is applied must be clean. After using, it should be thoroughly washed with turpentine or gasoline, and then several times with soap and hot water. Liquid soap, if available, is excellent for this purpose. After thoroughly rinsing in hot water, the brush should be laid in a dust-free place to dry. If it is not to be used for some time, it may then be wrapped in waxed paper until needed. This treatment will keep a brush soft and serviceable for a long time.

9. It never pays to buy a cheap varnish. The highest-priced varnish may be the cheapest in the end. Once the seal on a can of varnish has been broken, it cannot be kept for too long a period of time, as the quality will deteriorate.

10. When a varnish finish is used, a very thin coat of shellac should be applied over the stained and filled surface first. This prevents the stain from bleeding into the varnish.

As for the technique of applying stains, shellac, varnishes, etc., the general rule, with but a few exceptions, is as follows:

Beginning at the far edge of the surface, the finish must be brushed on evenly from one end to the other in the direction of the grain. Next, a strip adjacent to the first should be brushed on, and so on, until the entire surface has been covered. The brush must be kept well loaded to insure an even, fully covered surface.

The final operation in the finishing process is rubbing it down. When the final coat of shellac or varnish has been applied and is thoroughly dry and hard, it should be rubbed down with pumice stone and oil, or pumice stone and water. Powdered pumice stone can be bought at any paint or drug store for a few cents a pound. Rubbing oil also is very cheap and can be bought at all paint stores or painter's supply houses. Some powdered pumice stone should be placed in a shallow dish, and some of the oil poured into another shallow dish. Then after dipping a piece of rubbing felt first into the oil, and then into the pumice stone, the finished surface should be rubbed with firm, long strokes. Rubbing felt is about ¼ inch or more thick, and a piece about 3 by 5 inches will do very well. If it cannot be obtained, a piece of muslin folded several times will be a good substitute. Pumice stone and water cut faster and the surface will be left more dull than the surface rubbed with pumice stone and oil. However, the white powder that is left after water-rubbing is more difficult to remove than traces of pumice left when oil is used. The rubbing should be done until all high places have been leveled down and all shiny spots made dull. (Some finishers go over the piece with very fine steel wool before the pumice-stone rub.) The result, when the oil has been carefully wiped off, is a beautiful velvety finish.

If a shellacked surface has been rubbed, it should be gone over with a coat of beeswax to preserve it. See the problem on the Bannister-Back Side Chair (p. 63) for directions to prepare beeswax. Varnish does not need this protection. If a high polish is desired, the pumice-stone rub should be followed with a rub of rotten-stone and oil after about one week has elapsed.

When refinishing a piece of furniture, proceed in the following manner: Obtain a paint-and-varnish remover that dries very slowly, and flow it on the surface to be cleaned. After allowing it to soak for about 10 minutes, flow on a second application. Then with a stiff, short-bristle brush rub it briskly. After a short time, clean off the surface and repeat the operation. Proceed in this manner until all the old finish has been removed. Then wash thoroughly with gasoline, at least twice. Do this before the surface has had time to dry.

Allow the cleaned surface to dry for a period of 24 hours, and fill in all holes and nicks with stick shellac or plastic wood. Make all necessary repairs, and then proceed as with new work. Stick shellac is made in a variety of colors. Use the color that is as near the finish to be applied as possible. Heat a putty knife over an alcohol torch or a candle flame. Melt a tiny particle of the stick shellac on one corner of the heated putty knife, and apply it to the hole or crevice before it hardens. Smooth all rough spots with fine sandpaper.

INDEX